orship

Democracy and Dictatorship

The Nature and Limits of State Power

Norberto Bobbio

Translated by Peter Kennealy

University of Minnesota Press, Minneapolis

First published as *Stato, governo, società: Per una teoria generale
della politica*. Copyright © 1978, 1980, 1981, and, in the
collection, 1985 by Giulio Einaudi editore s.p.a., Torino

Published by the University of Minnesota Press
2037 University Avenue Southeast, Minneapolis   MN 55414.

Printed in Great Britain by TJ Press Ltd, Padstow

Library of Congress Catalog Card Number 89–051302

The University of Minnesota
is an equal-opportunity
educator and employer.

Contents

Introduction: Democracy and the Decline of the Left

by John Keane

THE DECLINE OF THE LEFT

What does it mean to be on the Left today? Few questions are so theoretically and politically significant – and so utterly perplexing. Only the origins of the term 'Left' seem uncontroversial.

It is well known that the idea of the Left is a child of the French Revolution – a metaphorical extension of the seating plan of the 1789 French Estates General, which became divided by the heated debates on the royal veto, with the 'third Estate' sitting to the King's left and the nobility to his right. It is also common knowledge that the idea of the Left played a critical role in nineteenth-century politics. It heightened the perception of the body politic as a broken continuum, as permanently divided by competing attitudes towards social change and political order. In opposition to the foot-dragging conservatism of the Right, with its haughty belief in the need for strict order and social control, Leftists were progressives. They optimistically embraced a faith in science, rationality and industry. They proclaimed their love of liberty and equality, and appealed to the essential goodness and sociability of human nature. The Left sympathized with the downtrodden. It despised the rich and powerful. It denounced parliamentary democracy as a bourgeois institution. It battled for a world freed from the evils of capitalism, material scarcity and unhappiness.

Since the First World War, this classical image of the Left has been crumbling slowly. The Left has become more cautious about modernity. It is less magnetized by the myths of scientific-technical progress and, especially within its green fringes, it has become openly hostile to industrialism; by contrast, it is the Right, from Mussolini to Thatcher, which has abandoned its former nostalgia and circumspection, and pressed home revolutionary or reformist policies based on a deep faith in scientific and economic modernization. In the same period, the levelling image of the Left has been damaged badly by its association with the cruel Stalinist programme of destroying liberty, equality and solidarity by means of cunning, violence, blood and terror – in Spain, in the Moscow trials, the Hitler–Stalin pact, Katyn and the military invasions of Hungary and Czechoslovakia. In consequence, the Left has become widely identified with the mastery of the skills of the lion and the fox, with the passion for political power and the wholesale politicization of personal and social life.

The Left's founding image of international class solidarity and opposition to state violence has also taken a severe beating. The rise of national communist regimes (as in Yugoslavia, China and Vietnam) has demonstrated that Leftism is not synonymous with selfless internationalism. Severe tensions among these regimes – the Maoist denunciation of Soviet 'revisionism' as a right-wing betrayal of communism is a dramatic case in point – and the more recent outbreak of war between these states (as in Indochina) have served to reinforce the image of the Left as a purveyor of self-interested power politics – as a mirror image of its right-wing opponents.

In recent years, the meaning of the term 'Left' has fallen into deeper disarray, especially in the countries of the West. It has become a muddled label which often obscures more than it clarifies. The appearance of the New Left at the end of the 1950s is one source of this trend. The willingness of many Left governments and parties after 1945 to embrace the 'mixed economy' and their more recent fascination with market mechanisms, the profit motive and small business has further blurred its distinctively 'left' qualities. Matters have been worsened by the confused reaction of trade unions, once considered the 'natural' heartland of Left support, to the failure of Keynesian reflationary policies. This confusion has been multiplied by deindustrialization, the growth of a new underclass and the emergence of more 'flexible' technologies, production methods and consumer styles. The western Left's loss of direction can also be traced to its nostalgic defence of centralized state bureaucracy and outdated techniques of management and planning. The conventional belief on the Left that state planning and fixing of markets plus selective nationalization plus spending money equals socialism has come unstuck. And the consequent tendency of some parts of the Left to display more pride in the past than faith in the future has been exacerbated by its intellectual torpor – its bad habit of submitting to the hypnotic powers of the Right, of repeating clichés and making politics through conventional labels.

The writings of Norberto Bobbio, Italy's leading political thinker, are an important reaction to this deep impasse of the Left. His work is pathbreaking because he sees the demand for more democracy as the key to a successful redefinition of the Left. What does democracy mean in this context? Bobbio's unusual 'liberal socialist' understanding of the term has been shaped by his early experiences in the liberal intellectual milieu of Turin in the 1930s, his deep involvement in the anti-Fascist Resistance, his subsequent intellectual and journalistic dialogues with the Italian Left, especially the PCI, and his current role as Life Senator and independent *franc-tireur* within Italian parliamentary politics.[1] Against the backdrop of such experiences, Bobbio insists – in the face of its twentieth-century vulgarization – that the concept of democracy is not elastic. It is not a word which can be made to mean whatever we choose it to mean. Democracy is understood by him as a system of procedural rules which specify *who* is authorized to make collective decisions and through which *procedures* such decisions are to be made. In contrast to all forms of heteronomous government, democracy comprises procedures for arriving at collective decisions in a way which secures the fullest possible participation of interested parties. At a minimum, according to Bobbio, democratic procedures include equal and universal adult suffrage; majority rule and guarantees of minority rights, which ensure that collective decisions are approved by a substantial number of those expected to make them; the rule of law; and constitutional guarantees of freedom of assembly and expression and other liberties, which help guarantee that those expected to decide or to elect those who decide can choose among real alternatives.

Democracy in this sense is a method of preventing those who govern from permanently appropriating power for their own ends. Those exercising power are subject to procedures which enable others to question, rotate or sack them. The distribution of power in democratic systems tends to reflect the outcomes of political contests framed by permanent decision-making rules. Conflict and compromise are therefore institutionalized, and power becomes secular and 'disembodied'. It is not permanently consubstantial with any particular individual or group – a monarch, for instance – but is exercised instead by flesh-and-blood mortals who are subject to removal and are accountable to others, in accordance with the rules of the democratic game.

Bobbio argues that in general the present-day Left has either muddled or no clear ideas about the importance and nature of the rules of democracy, and in particular whether to reform or replace them. This leads him to challenge several standard Leftist misconceptions about democracy. For example, Bobbio is adamant that the historical emergence of liberal democratic institutions, such as free elections, competitive party systems and written constitutions, represented a great leap forward in the fight for more

democracy. Liberal democratic institutions are not necessarily a device for protecting the class interests of the
bourgeoisie. Liberal democracy (to paraphrase Lenin) is
not the best political shell for capitalism. Liberal democratic
institutions are in fact an indispensable bulwark against the
unending arrogance of political actors, a vital mechanism
for limiting the scope and haughtiness of state power. A
post-liberal democracy is thinkable and desirable, but a
non-liberal democracy is a contradiction in terms and in
fact.

Bobbio is also adamant that the friends of democracy
must reject the bad 'New Left' habit of calling for the
disappearance of all organization and its replacement by
so-called spontaneous action. A democratic polity without
procedural rules is not only a contradiction in terms. It is
also a recipe for arbitrary decision-making and misgovern-
ment. The friends of democracy must also recognize that
the full replacement of representative forms of democracy
by participatory, direct democracy – which require (in the
case of decisions affecting the whole polity) the public
assembly of millions of citizens – is technically impossible
in large-scale, complex societies. Direct democracy, the
participation of citizens in the *agora*, is suited only to small
states and organizatons in which 'the people find it easy to
meet and in which every citizen can easily get to know all
the others' (Rousseau). More controversially, Bobbio argues
that the attempt to foist the principle of direct democracy
on to representative institutions – for instance, applying a
binding mandate to elected parliamentary 'delegates' – is
undesirable, since it contradicts the principle, indispensable
in any parliamentary democracy, that representatives represent general rather than narrowly sectional interests and
therefore require some powers to negotiate freely and to
act independently of those whom they represent.

Bobbio emphasizes the important point that direct
democracy thrives upon consensual decision-making, and
that it therefore works best when there are a limited number
of alternative policy choices – nuclear power or no nuclear

power, peace or war, or the legalization or criminalization of abortion. Otherwise, the trust, patience and mutual support that are required within self-governing circles are often overburdened with multiple and conflicting points of view, the tensions among which cannot be resolved easily without the presence of intermediaries – that is, without institutions of delegated or representative democracy which 'filter out' and simplify the kaleidoscope of conflicting opinions.

This is not to say that representative, parliamentary democracy is the alpha and omega of political forms. Bobbio recognizes, correctly, that the representative system is constrained and limited by accumulations of *social* power within civil society. The vast majority of citizens has no say in major decisions concerning economic investment, production and growth. Churches, trade unions and many other institutions of civil society remain insufficiently democratic. Exactly how more democracy within the sphere of civil society might be achieved in practice is unclear from Bobbio's account. He refers only to the need to develop, broaden and reinforce all the institutions from which modern democracy was born. Priority should be given, in his view, to the task of supplementing political democracy with 'social democracy' – extending the process of democratization from the political sphere (where individuals are regarded as citizens) to the civil sphere, where individuals are regarded variously as men and women, entrepreneurs and workers, teachers and students, producers and consumers. Struggles over *where* citizens can vote should be given as much priority as the struggles in the nineteenth and early twentieth centuries over *who* can vote.

Bobbio emphasizes that in practice this refinement and extension of democracy – broadening the domains *where* citizens can vote – does not require all individuals to play the role of fulltime political animals. Too much democracy can kill off democracy. The wholesale politicization of life, the attempt to create a society of fulltime, omnicompetent citizens, is in fact antithetical to democracy. It would produce hellish and unworkable results – everything would be defined as political, private life would be swallowed up by the public sphere, human beings would be transformed, perhaps forcibly, into 'total citizens', despite the fact that the growing diversification and complexity of modern societies prevents individual citizens from being in the same place at the same time to make decisions which affect their lives directly or indirectly. Free time would become a thing of the past. The life of the fulltime, omnicompetent citizen would be a nightmare of interminable meetings, endless negotiations and late-night telephone calls. Moreover, according to Bobbio, Europeans are heirs of an historical tradition in which state power is supposed to be limited in favour of non-state spheres, such as religious communities, households, centres of learning and research, and markets.

This historically felt need to limit the scope and power of the state is a central and distinctive feature of Bobbio's attempt to redefine the meaning of Left politics. He views state power as necessary and yet corruptible and dangerous, and as therefore in need of preventive measures and effective defences, such as a plurality of social forces and organizations which run parallel to the state. In Bobbio's view, the enormous problem which faces the Left is to know how to create through its own agency a state apparatus which is efficient without being oppressive or, in other words, which can function effectively as the agent of civil society without at the same time lapsing into a dictatorship.

THE GREAT DICHOTOMIES

This volume of connected essays – a small encyclopaedia of key political terms – is jam-packed with insights which bear on this problem. Consistent with Bobbio's dislike of obscure jargon and emotive slogans – his intellectual temperament is consistently sceptical and democratic and imbued with a sense of the complexity of things – these essays get down to the serious business of carefully analysing

classical, medieval and modern traditions of reflection on
the scope and limits of political action. The essays might
be described as an exercise in historical semantics – as an
attempt to reconstruct the changing meaning through time
of certain political keywords. This exercise is evidently
infinite in scope. There are always new texts to be read
and further illustrations to be developed, and both tasks
would in turn modify or amplify the conclusions already
reached. Bobbio meets this possible objection by concentrating on a number of key political terms and their opposites
– such as the public and the private, civil society and the
state, democracy and dictatorship – which hold the key to
resolving the problem of how to limit and control the
exercise of state power. His choice of certain pairs of
concepts ('great dichotomies' Bobbio calls them) reveals
his deep attachment to the tradition of modern liberal
constitutionalism, but it is no less unusual and stimulating
for that. It has the advantage of illuminating the origins,
shifting meanings and normative implications of each term
by comparing it with its partner. In this way, the structure
of any given political system or historical era can be better
understood by knowing what has been said or written about
it. For example, the *differentia specifica* of modern times
and its patterns of political thought when compared to its
classical and medieval counterparts can be better grasped,
and the rough and narrow paths of democratic theory can
be better negotiated.

The essays assembled in this volume are invaluable guides
in this adventure. To begin with, Bobbio examines the
public/private dichotomy. This contrast first entered the
history of western political thought for the purpose of
distinguishing between what belongs to a group as a
collectivity and what belongs to its single members or lesser
groupings like households and enterprises. The public/
private dichotomy in turn harbours other important distinctions, which Bobbio teases out with skill and patience: for
example, the distinction between associations of equals (as
in the *polis*) and communities of unequals (as in the *oikos*);

between the public law which is imposed by political authority and the private law which regulates the interaction of private persons in such matters as property, inheritance and marriage; and the distinction between the principles of distributive justice, which guide public authority in the distribution of honours and duties, and the principles of commutative justice, which cover buying and selling, labour contracts and other private individuals and groups considered to be of equal value.

Bobbio points out that the original distinction between the public and the private was ordered hierarchically, in that the public was affirmed as supreme in relation to the peripheral powers of the private. An example is the classic definition of Cicero of the *res publica* as an aggregation of people bonded together by the *utilitas communione*. This primacy of the public over the private was challenged successively, for example, by the diffusion of Roman law, whose principal institutions are property, contracts and the family. This trend was reinforced, ironically, by the development (by Bartolo di Sassoferrato, Jean Bodin and others) of a systematic body of public law during the first phases of development of the modern state. This hastened the questioning of the primacy of the public over the private by triggering disputes about whether the people have forever conceded or only temporarily entrusted power to the sovereign. During the seventeenth and eighteenth centuries the opposition of the private sphere to the public underwent a thorough 'modernization'. Locke and others argued for the inviolability of property in the lives, liberties and other natural rights of individuals. Even theorists of absolutism like Hobbes considered as unjust the sovereign who violated the property of his or her subjects. And prior to the French Revolution the exponents of political economy radically extended this liberal theory of the primacy of the private over the public. They emphasized the fundamental difference between the sphere of economic relations (understood as an ensemble of relationships among formally equal individuals who are in fact rendered unequal by the division of labour) and the sphere of political institutions – a distinction which powerfully reinforced the defence of civil society against the state during that period.

The 'great dichotomy' between civil society and the state features prominently in this volume. In today's political vocabulary, Bobbio points out, civil society refers to the sphere of social relations – households, communications media, markets, churches, voluntary organizations and social movements – which are not controlled directly by state institutions. It is widely understood as a defining characteristic of modern life. Civil society and the state are seen as two necessarily separate but contiguous and interdependent aspects of contemporary life. Bobbio emphasizes the novelty of this viewpoint. Well into the eighteenth century, European political thinkers understood civil society as a synonym for a type of political association whose members are subject to laws which ensure peaceful order and good government. This meaning of the term is traceable through Cicero's idea of *societas civilis* to the Aristotelean view that civil society (*koionia politike*) is that society, the *polis*, which contains and governs all others. According to Bobbio, this old custom of treating civil society as coterminous with the state was always under pressure from attempts, recurrent in Christian thought, to distinguish the area of competence of the civil powers from the domain of religious power. It was challenged directly for the first time by German writers (especially Marx and Hegel). For Hegel civil society is a moment in the process of the formation and completion of the State. It includes the market economy, social classes, corporations, and institutions whose transactions are regulated by civil law and, as such, are not directly dependent upon the political state itself. Marx's interpretation of Hegel's concept of civil society is by contrast reductive and ultimately distorted, in Bobbio's view. Marx's *bürgerliche Gesellschaft* referred to society in the sense of a class society riddled with bourgeois practices and assumptions. It is a product of an historical subject, the bourgeoisie, which legitimated its struggles against the absolutist state in the language of the rights of man and citizen, which in reality serves only the particular interests of the bourgeoisie.

Bobbio's treatment of the original and subsequent accounts of modern civil society – including that of Gramsci – arguably places too much emphasis on the German case and neglects the reticence of German thinkers about its democratic implications.[2] Bobbio nevertheless correctly underscores the wide range of conflicting meanings of the expression 'civil society' and its counterpart, the state. Bobbio shows that state institutions have often been viewed from a variety of standpoints. They can be treated as an aspect of the history of institutions or treated in terms of the history of political ideas or of normative political philosophy. The theme of the state can also be approached through the distinction between sociological and legal doctrines (a distinction emphasized in Georg Jellinek's *General Doctrine of the State (Allgemeine Staatslehre) 1910*); that is, the state can be viewed either as primarily a legally produced and legally governed entity or as a form of organization which cannot be dissociated from the ensemble of underlying social relations which condition or determine its functioning.

The historical appearance of the idea of the state in its modern form is attributed by Bobbio to such works as Machiavelli's *Prince* and Hobbes's *Leviathan*, where the state is understood as the supreme institutionalized power – the 'machine state' – that can be exercised over the inhabitants of a given territory. The state is defined as the bearer of the *summa potestas*; whoever has the exclusive power or right to use force on a given territory is considered sovereign. Whether this idea of the state – in contrast to the idea of the Greek *polis* and the Roman *res publica* – was entirely novel is a matter of deep controversy. According to Bobbio, some writers – Max Weber is among the most important – see the reality of the modern state, with its monopoly of the means of violence, administration and taxation, as unprecedented. Other writers – Machiavelli's close reading of Roman history in search of political examples applicable to the states of his time is an example – have been inclined to identify a measure of continuity between the systems of the ancient, medieval and modern worlds.

Theories of the state have also been marked by bitter controversies about the appropriate relationship between sovereign and subjects, rulers and ruled, the state and its citizens. This relationship has been defined by most political thinkers as a relationship between superiors and inferiors. The history of political thought, Bobbio's analysis shows, has been mainly a history written from above. The dominant tradition that runs from Plato's *Statesman* and Xenophon's *Cyropaedia* to Hobbes's *Leviathan* and Schmitt's *Die Diktatur* has represented political power from the standpoint of the rulers. It has sought to justify the power-holders' right to command and the subjects' duty to obey by defending various principles of legitimacy. These include the authority of God; the will of the people; nature (as an original force, *kratos*, or as the law of reason or modern natural law); appeals to history; or, as in legal positivism, references to the fact that law is made and enforced by authorities appointed by the political system itself. This dominant tradition has come under fire increasingly in modern times. The entitlements of the governed – the 'hidden side of the moon' of western political thought in Bobbio's words – have come ever more sharply in focus. The natural rights of the individual; the liberty, wealth and happiness of citizens; the right of resistance to unjust laws; the separation of powers; the rule of law; office-holding and law-making subject to time limits: these and other principles have been invoked in opposition to state-centred theories of politics. Such principles are seen to exist independently of political power, which is required both to respect and to protect them. The individual is not seen to be destined to serve the state. Rather, the state must serve the individual so that, as Spinoza put it, even sovereigns who can do anything they want are forced in practice to recognize that they cannot make a table eat grass.

The changing fortunes of the theory of dictatorship, analysed in the last essay in this volume, is an important example of the way in which the entitlements of the governed becomes an ever more prominent theme in modern political thought. From ancient to early modern thinkers (up to Rousseau, Babeuf and Buonarrotti) the institution of dictatorship was distinguished by its exceptional and temporary character. 'Dictator' was originally the name of the Roman magistrate to whom extraordinary powers were legitimately given in times of war or domestic revolt. Bobbio points out that the idea that dictatorship is required periodically to stabilize an existing order comes under heavy fire in modern times. In this era of great revolutionary upheavals, the concept of dictatorship is extended to include regimes which aim to change the world, to smash the old order, and to establish a brand new regime. The modern idea of dictatorship – Buonarrotti's committee of 'wise and enlightened' men who boldly guide the revolution is an example – is further distinguished from its classical counterpart by the insistence that not only the powers of the executive but *all* state functions should be mobilized in support of dictatorship. During the nineteenth century, the originally positive connotations of the term dictatorship were also dissolved. Marx, Engels and others considered *every* state to be dictatorial. Dictatorship was denounced as 'domination', as a necessary and enduring feature of the exercise of all forms of political power. According to Bobbio, this shift away from a positive to a negative definition of dictatorship is even more marked during the twentieth century. From the time of the fiery debates about the nature of the Bolshevik and fascist regimes, dictatorship and democracy are seen to be antithetical forms of government. Dictatorship is widely regarded with suspicion or disdain. It comes to mean all undemocratic ways of wielding power.

Although Bobbio notes – approvingly – that democracy is today still generally reckoned to be preferable to dictatorship, he is not starry-eyed about its merits and advantages. Certainly, he considers democracy the chief antidote of dictatorship and violent politics, which are potentially inherent in the operation of all modern states. In the final analysis, these states rest on a foundation of armed force. This means not only that the danger of war and the militarization of civil society is omnipresent in the field of inter-state relations, but also that the political leaders of each nation-state continually have access to its irreducibly violent potential. Whenever they are challenged or wish to accumulate further power, political leaders can resort to institutions such as the police and the military, which are deeply antithetical to democracy because they thrive on secrecy, cunning, enforced unanimity and, ultimately, the shout to arms and the crash of hobnailed boots on the pavement.

By contrast, democratic procedures are based on non-violent, open negotiations and revocable compromises, and for this reason Bobbio considers them more 'civilized'. Yet his enthusiasm for democracy is controlled. It does not treat democracy as a synonym for the 'good life' (Lipset). A unique feature of Bobbio's defence of democracy is its honest concern with the *limits* of democracy. He emphasizes several of these limits. While the democratic method is treated as a precious and vital human invention, he insists that it is not always and everywhere a viable mode of decision-making. Bobbio does not repeat the oldest (and old hat) arguments against democracy, for instance that democracy always degenerates into lawlessness and licence, so that the father fears his son and 'the master fears and flatters his pupils and the pupils laugh at their masters and teachers' (Plato). Bobbio instead illustrates his thesis about the limits of democracy with reference to periods of crisis, such as war, violent upheaval and domestic 'states of emergency', in which democratic rules of the game rarely apply. (Whether they *can* or *should* be made to apply is a different problem, left untreated by Bobbio.) In such periods, social and political outcomes are determined by self-interested calculation and bloody struggles for power over others. The basic rules of democracy seem to be an unaffordable luxury.

Bobbio also sees the democratic method to be threatened by a number of *irreversible* historical trends. For example, the extension of the suffrage and the growth of social demands on the liberal democratic state have forced it to expand its functions and services and – the Weberian roots of Bobbio's argument are here strongly evident – to administer these services through a constantly expanding bureaucratic apparatus which is structured hierarchically and not democratically. Bobbio further claims that the number of problems requiring technical expertise and professional solutions is rising, and that this reduces the applicability of the democratic principle that everyone can decide everything. Inevitably, government by technicians spreads. Citizens' (potential) sovereignty is whittled away in favour of *qualunquismo*, the apathy and indifference of private beings who are interested only in cultivating their gardens. Finally, Bobbio laments the undemocratic and atomizing impact of the mass media. He points out that democracy presupposes the free and full development of the faculties of individual citizens, and yet he claims that this requirement is violated daily by the manipulative appeals of the press and broadcasting media, which diminish the space reserved for informed judgements by stimulating convictions based on either fleeting emotions or the passive imitation of others – all in the name of 'popular choice'. The abstract principle of popular sovereignty is thereby translated into reality in debased form.

Bobbio's account of the limits of democracy is arguably incomplete and less than convincing. There is much evidence that the 'irreversible' historical trends alleged by Bobbio are in fact highly *contingent* developments. Bureaucratic organizations certainly tend to reduce their members and clients to mere objects of administrative control, but they

also typically stimulate the growth of independent public
spheres by depending on a measure of initiative from their
members and by feigning acceptance of the principle of
mediating conflicting interests through controversy, open
discussion, compromise and consensus. Bobbio's defence
of the principle of government by technicians is also
questionable. Complex organizations cannot operate auto-
matically, that is, guided only by technical knowledge and
procedures. Human skill, improvisation and collective
judgements are essential for preventing them from regularly
malfunctioning in unexpected and often dangerous ways.
The introduction of the most advanced machine systems
(such as computers and robots) into complex organizations
further increases the number of open-ended and unstruc-
tured problems, which cannot be solved by technical
expertise alone but only with the co-operation of those who
work directly with these new information technologies. And
the astonishing capacity of these technologies to alter
flexibly both the range of products and rhythms of work
can be managed only through collective human decisions
at the point of production. Finally, the emphasis placed by
Bobbio on the atomizing and depoliticizing effects of the
mass media is one-sided. It neglects the serious political
controversies which have erupted in recent decades between
the supporters of state-regulated and market-regulated press
and audio-visual media; and it neglects the ways in which
most citizens – as the remarkable growth of video piracy
and the illegal use of descramblers suggest – today retain
a native (if undeveloped) capacity to select, reinterpret,
criticize, or – like tortoises – shield themselves completely
against the appeals of the mass media.[3]

Bobbio's examination of the limitations of democracy is
also arguably incomplete. There are quite a number of
weaknesses inherent in the democratic method – they range
from old doubts about democracy's lack of philosophical
self-confidence to new concerns about the inability of
democratic procedures to resolve such dilemmas as that
between the growing power of human control over nature

and the growing need of the human species to give institutional recognition to our fundamental dependence upon nature itself – and its friends need urgently to discuss them, if only to defend democracy against its harshest critics. Admittedly, this is a controversial undertaking. Some democrats insist that to interrogate the democratic method is to erode its credibility and destroy its self-confidence. This conviction is mistaken. The long-term survival of democracy must involve anticipating the objections of its critics, honestly exploring the dilemmas and paradoxes which riddle democratic politics, thereby recognizing that democracy cannot achieve certain things. Democratic theory must state issues it knows it cannot resolve; it must attempt to hold up a mirror, admittedly somewhat clouded, to look at itself in. Bobbio attempts to do exactly this, and his key point is well taken. The democratic method does indeed have clear limits, which should serve as a warning against attempts to build a perfect democracy. Like the behaviour of the daughters of Pelia, who tried to rejuvenate their aging father by hacking him to pieces, attempts to perfect democracy endanger democracy itself.

And yet even though democracy has endemic limits, Bobbio is adamant that the democratic method generally remains superior to all other dictatorial methods of decision-making. Why does Bobbio sympathize with this method – despite the fact that in the history of political thought democracy has had many more enemies than friends? Why does he consider the democratization of the Left – its unconditional embrace of the democratic method – of paramount importance? In short, why is democracy a good thing?

Bobbio discusses several types of responses to these questions, although his list is less complete and more conventional than might be expected. For example, Bobbio emphasizes that the most important feature of democratic procedures is that they enable the approval of decisions of interest to the whole collectivity, or at least a majority of citizens. This overlooks the key point – still inadequately recognized in democratic theory – that democratic procedures also enable the *disapproval* and *revision* of established agreements, and that for this reason they are uniquely suited to complex western societies. Democratic procedures are superior to all other types of decision-making not because they guarantee both a consensus and 'good' decisions, but because they provide citizens who are affected by certain decisions with the possibility of reconsidering their judgements about the quality and unintended consequences of these decisions. Democratic procedures increase the level of 'flexibility' and 'reversibility' of decision-making. They encourage incremental learning and trial-and-error modification (or 'muddling through'), and that is why they are best suited to the task of publicly monitoring and controlling (and sometimes shutting down) complex and tightly coupled 'high-risk' organizations, whose failure (as in Bhopal, Three-Mile Island and Chernobyl) can have catastrophic ecological and social consequences. Democracy is an unrivalled remedy for technocratic delusions. It is an indispensable means of making accountable those who turn a blind eye to the 'normal accidents' which plague high-risk systems, and who seek to define acceptable levels of risk by means of technical analyses of probability – or simply by falling back on the childish solipsism that whatever isn't believed couldn't possibly be harmful.

Only democratic procedures can openly and fairly select certain kinds of dangers for public attention, carefully monitor and bring to heel those responsible for managing risky organizations, thereby minimizing the possibility of error and reducing the chances of the big mistake. Unfortunately, Bobbio does not consider this unusual line of reasoning. He instead examines three more conventional types of arguments for democracy. The first and weakest of these is the utilitarian argument that democracy is superior to dictatorship because it enables the best interpreters of interests – the interested parties themselves – to sift through various options and to decide for themselves. Aside from the probability that interested individuals and groups confuse their short-term and longer-run interests because they often see no further than their own noses, the utilitarian argument mistakenly assumes that the collective interest is only ever the sum of individual interests. A second and more convincing type of argument, according to Bobbio, is that democratic procedures maximize freedom in the sense of autonomy. Why autonomy is a good thing is unclear from Bobbio's account; he simply assumes that it is one of those ultimate values which cannot be deduced rationally. If freedom (to paraphrase Rousseau) is obedience to the laws which citizens formulate and apply to themselves then democratic procedures for arriving at collective decisions through the fullest possible participation of interested parties is a natural ally of autonomy.

Finally, and most importantly, Bobbio considers the view that democracy is superior because it remains the strongest antidote to the abuse of power. He endorses Montesquieu's maxim that those who exercise power always want more of it and for more extended periods. The great advantage of democracy is that it is a type of decision-making procedure which monitors itself through its own agency. A bad democracy is for this reason always better than a good dictatorship. Democracy is a self-reflexive means of controlling the exercise of power, and it is for this reason an indispensable weapon in the fight to interrogate, restrict and to dissolve dictatorial power. Democrats are certainly not exempted from this democratic equation. Democrats seek to alter radically and to equalize the existing distribution of power within and between the state and civil society. They are normally confronted with various acts of sabotage and resistance by their opponents and, hence, faced with the temptation of overcoming such obstacles by accumulating ever more power. The lust for power knows no political affiliation. It is polymorphously perverse. It requires constant correction and eternal vigilance.

This rule applies especially to those who consider themselves as heirs to a socialist version of the classical

Left project. In capitalist society – according to Marx and others – the institutional bases of class power and state power are differentiated. The separation of political and social forms of stratification is seen (correctly) to be a unique feature of the modern bourgeois era. The human species is subdivided for the first time into *social* classes; individuals' legal status is divorced from their socio-economic role within civil society; each individual is sundered into both private egoist and public-spirited citizen; and civil society, the realm of private needs and interests, waged labour and private right, is emancipated from political control, and becomes the basis and presupposition of the state. Civil society is also the power base of the leading class, the bourgeoisie, which is the first 'non-political' class in human history. Its control of civil society ensures that political power is normally a secondary or derivative phenomenon; the state is an instrument for protecting and managing the political affairs of the bourgeoisie and its allies.

The socialist project aimed to undo this development by abolishing the social power of the bourgeoisie and, hence, destroying the division between civil society and the state. The problem, according to Bobbio, is that state power tends to become dictatorial whenever it ceases to be subject to the countervailing powers of civil society. And that is not the only problem. If socialism means a society in which ownership of the means of production has been transferred from private hands into the laps of 'society' – in the twentieth century that has normally meant the state itself – then the abuses of state power are (and have been) much more likely than in a capitalist society. Under socialist conditions, citizens would be exposed constantly to the whims and calculations of a state which simultaneously performed the functions of policeman, administrator, social worker *and* employer.

Bobbio's argument here comes full circle. It emphasizes, rightly, that the demand for socialism in the conventional sense is undemocratic; and that the demand for democracy is much more subversive because it calls into question all heteronomous forms of power. This is why Bobbio insists that the democratization of the Left, its militant defence of the democratic method, is of fundamental contemporary importance. He concludes that the Left needs democracy in order to live up to its old promises of greater equality and solidarity *with* liberty; and that, in view of the systematic failure of the Left to keep these promises, its full acceptance of the democratic method would radically alter the methods, policies and public image of the Left. It would become a synonym for the democratic fight for greater democracy.

While this proposed redefinition of the Left is tentative and its policy implications sketchy, its deep political significance should not be underestimated. Once or twice in each century whole political spectrums break up and undergo massive realignment. We are living through one of these painful and topsy-turvy periods of readjustment, and Bobbio's writings help to explain why. His arguments expose several key blindspots and muddles of the Left. They help to clarify the advantages and disadvantages of the democratic method. And they deepen our appreciation of the unexpected global upsurge of the democratic revolution at the end of the twentieth century – in Poland and Hungary, Brazil and Argentina, the Philippines and China. Bobbio's arguments will nevertheless irritate many orthodox Leftists, especially those who continue to defend the primacy of 'socialism' and who consequently fail to see that the citizen has problems distinct from those of the worker or consumer, and that political and social democracy cannot be resolved into economic democracy. For those who remain flippant about the advantages of democracy, or who turn a blind eye to the ways in which contemporary western democracies are fragile, corruptible and often corrupt – those who haven't yet seen that the middle of the political road is often a dead end – Bobbio's writings should be compulsory reading. And for smug neo-conservatives, who pronounce the death of the Left by implosion,

these writings should serve as a warning that the imagination
of a new democratic Left has begun to stir.

Notes

1   The historical and intellectual context of Bobbio's political
    thinking is well discussed in Perry Anderson, 'The Affinities
    of Norberto Bobbio', *New Left Review* 170 (July/August 1988),
    pp. 3–36, and Richard Bellamy, *Modern Italian Social Theory*,
    Cambridge 1987, chapter 8.
2   See my 'Despotism and Democracy. The Origins and Develop-
    ment of the Distinction Between Civil Society and the State
    1750–1850', in John Keane (ed.), *Civil Society and the State,
    New European Perspectives*, London and New York 1988.
3   These points concerning bureaucracy, new information techno-
    logies and the mass media are elaborated in my *Public Life
    and Late Capitalism*, New York and London 1984; Charles
    Perrow, *Normal Accidents, Living with High-Risk Technolog-
    ies*, New York 1984; and my '"Liberty of the Press" in the
    1990s', *New Formations* 8 (Summer 1989), pp. 34–52.

Preface

Four pieces are brought together in this volume without any significant changes from when they were first written for the *Enciclopedia Einaudi*. These are 'Democracy and Dictatorship' from Volume IV (1978), 'Public/Private' from Volume XI (1980), 'Civil Society' and 'State' from Volume XII (1981). These are closely connected themes and I apologize to the reader in advance for any inevitable repetitions. The first and the second are presented directly in the form of antitheses, while the third and the fourth deal individually with the terms of another antithesis which is no less crucial in the history of political thought: civil society/state.

One of the guiding principles of the encyclopaedia, the analysis of certain key terms together with their opposites, was particularly congenial to me. In 1974 I had written an article on the classical distinction between private law and public law and I called it 'The Great Dichotomy'. The antithesis democracy/dictatorship reproduces in ordinary language the philosophical contrast between autonomy and heteronomy that goes back through Kelsen to Kant and which I have often reproposed. I had already examined the antithesis civil society/state, historically in the works of Hegel, Marx and Gramsci, and analytically in the *Dizionario Politico* (published by UTET) under the title 'Civil Society'.

Dealing with antitheses offers the advantage at the descriptive level of light being thrown on one term by the other, and it is often the case that the weak term is defined as the negation of the strong term (private as non-public, for example); evaluatively it allows one to highlight the positive or negative judgement which, depending on the author, falls on one or other of the two terms as, for instance, in the ancient dispute about whether democracy or autocracy is preferable. In its historical use it can even be employed to outline a philosophy of history, for example, in the changeover from an era of the primacy of private law to an era of the primacy of public law.

The longest by far of the four pieces is 'State, Power and Government', which is a reprint of 'State'. It summarizes and synthesizes in part the other three. I conceived it as an attempt, I do not know how successful, to cover the vast area of the problems of the state looked at from the legal and political viewpoints, which are often separated; or, in other words, of the state as a legal system and as a sovereign power. In that piece I examined certain ideas, especially regarding power, its various forms and the different criteria of legitimation which I had never before exposed with such thoroughness. The other essays, however, are reworkings of earlier or more recent pieces: 'The Great Dichotomy: Public/Private' goes back partly to 'Public–Private – introduction to a debate' (1982) and partly to 'Democracy and Invisible Power' (1980). 'Civil Society' goes back to, as well as the writings already cited, the essay 'On the Notion of Civil Society' (1968). 'Democracy and Dictatorship' is taken largely from 'The Theory of Governmental Forms in the History of Political Thought' (1976).

These are themes on which I have often worked in the past ten years: together they form a fragment of a general theory of politics yet to be written.

Norberto Bobbio

1

The Great Dichotomy:
Public/Private

A DICHOTOMOUS PAIR

It was in two much commented-on passages of Justinian's
Corpus iuris (*Institutiones*, 1, 1, 4; *Digesto*, 1, 1, 1, 2)
where public law and private law are defined in an identical
manner – the first as *quod ad statum rei romanae spectat*,
and the second as *quod ad singulorum utilitatem* – that the
pair of terms 'public' and 'private' first entered the history
of Western political and social thought. Through constant
and continuous use, and without any substantial changes,
they have since become one of the 'great dichotomies' used
by several disciplines – social and historical sciences as well
as law – to define, represent and order their particular
fields of investigation. In this respect the dichotomy can be
likened to others playing a similar role in the social sciences:
war/peace, democracy/autocracy, society/community, state
of nature/civil society. A great dichotomy may correctly be
spoken of when we are confronted with a distinction that
is suitable (a) for dividing a world into two spheres which
together are exhaustive in the sense that every element of
that world is covered, and mutually exclusive in the
sense that any element covered by the first term cannot
simultaneously be covered by the second; and (b) for
establishing a division that is not only comprehensive in
the sense that all elements potentially or actually referred
to by the discipline are covered by it, but also dominant in

that it subsumes other distinctions and makes them second-ary. In legal language, the pre-eminence of the distinction between private and public law over all other distinctions, its unchanging use in different historical periods and its comprehensiveness were sufficient to make a neo-Kantian philosophy of law treat the two concepts of private and public law as two a priori categories of legal thinking (Radbruch 1932, 122–7).

The terms of a dichotomy can either be defined indepen-dently of each other, or else only one is defined while the other is defined negatively with respect to it (peace as not-war). In this latter case, the first term is said to be the dominant one and the second the weak one. The definition of public law and private law mentioned above is an example of the first case, although the first term is stronger in that private is often defined as 'not-public' (*privatus qui in magistratu non est*, Forcellini), and rarely the other way around. In addition, it can be said that the two terms of a dichotomy qualify each other in the sense they always occur together: in legal language, public law suggests instantly, by contrast, private contract, for example. In ordinary language the public interest is determined with respect to and by contrast with private interest and vice versa. Finally, from the moment that the space defined by the two terms is completely covered (*tertium non datur*) they arrive at the point of mutually defining themselves in the sense that the public domain extends only as far as the start of the private sphere (and the reverse is also true). The size of the areas referred to by either of the terms can be enlarged or reduced depending on the situation to which the dichotomy is applied. One of the commonplaces of the age-old debate about the relationship between the public and private domains is that increasing the size of the public sphere reduces the private sphere and vice versa, an assertion which is generally accompanied and complicated by contrast-ing value judgements.

Whatever the origin of the distinction or the moment of its birth, the classic dichotomy between public and private law reflects the situation of a group which distinguishes between what belongs to the group as a group and what belongs to single members or, more generally, between the society as a whole and other incidental, lesser groupings (such as the family) or else between a superior central power and inferior peripheral powers which enjoy only a relative autonomy, if any. In fact, the original distinction between public and private was accompanied by an affirmation of the supremacy of the first over the second, as is shown by one of the fundamental principles which regulates every arrangement covered by the great division: the principle according to which *ius publicum privatorum pactis mutari non potest* (*Digesto*, 38, 2, 14) or *privatorum conventio iuri publico non derogat* (ibid., 45, 50, 17). Notwithstanding the age-old debate provoked by the variety of criteria which justify – or which are held to justify – the division of the two spheres, the fundamental criterion remains that of the different persons and situations to which the general notion of *utilitas* applies. Besides the *singulorum utilitas* of the definition already cited, the celebrated Ciceronian definition of the *res publica* should not be forgotten: a 'thing of the people', when 'people' means not just an aggregation of individuals but a society held together by the *utilitatis communione* (*De re publica*, 1, 41, 48) as well as by legal bonds.

CORRESPONDING DICHOTOMIES

The conceptual, classificatory and evaluative relevance of the public/private dichotomy is demonstrated by the fact that it includes other traditional and recurring dichotomies of the social sciences that both converge in it and fill it out, but which can also replace it.

Associations of equals and associations of unequals

Since the law is an ordering of social relations the great public/private dichotomy is primarily reflected in the distinction between two types of social relationships: between equals and between unequals. The state – and any other organized society with either a total or partial public sphere – is characterized by relations of subordination between governors and governed, or rather between holders of the power of command and subjects with the duty of obedience. These are relationships of inequality. Both natural society (as described by natural lawyers) and market society (as idealized by the classical economists in which the private sphere is opposed to the public sphere) are characterized by relationships of coordination between equals. The distinction between an association of equals and an association of unequals is no less classic than the distinction between public and private spheres. Thus Vico writes: *Omnis societas omino duplex, inaequalis et aequalis* (1720, ch. LX). The family, the state, and the relations between God and man are found amongst the first; amongst the second are found associations of brothers, kin, friends, citizens, guests and enemies.

It can be seen from examples that the two dichotomies of public/private and society of equals/society of unequals do not completely overlap; conventionally, the family belongs to the private sphere as opposed to the public sphere; or rather it is placed in the private sphere where it is towered over by the more complex organization of the city (in the Aristotelian sense of the word) or the state (in the sense of modern political writers). However, with respect to the difference beteween the two types of association, the family is an association of unequals. Evidence that the family belongs to the private sphere is provided by the fact that the European public law which accompanied the foundation of the modern constitutional state placed in the private sphere those patriarchal, paternalistic and despotic conceptions of sovereign power which liken the state to a family writ large or those which attribute to the sovereign the powers of the patriarch, the father or the master: all positions of different strength in family associations. Vico, on the other hand, saw the relations between enemies as relations of equality – correctly, apart from anything else, because international society is, abstractly considered, an association of formally equal entities, so much so that Hobbes and Hegel compare it to the state of nature – and they usually belong to the realm of public law, if only the external public law governing the relations between states rather than the internal public law governing the relations between ruler and ruled in the same state.

With the birth of political economy which gave rise to the differentiation of the sphere of economic relations from the sphere of political relations, economic relations were substantially understood as relations between unequals (as a result of the division of labour) but formally equal in the market. The public/private dichotomy reappeared in the form of the distinction between political society (of unequals) and economic society (of equals). From the point of view of the agent characteristic of each, a distinction was made between the society of the *citoyen* who attends to the public interest, and that of the *bourgeois* who takes care of his or her own private interests in competition or collaboration with other individuals. Behind the distinction between the economic sphere and the political sphere is the ancient distinction between the *singulorum utilitas* and the *status rei publicae*, and through it public and private spheres were differentiated for the first time. Thus, with the birth of political economy, the natural law distinction between the state of nature and civil society is rehabilitated in the distinction between economic society and political society. Soon after that civil society, understood in a Hegelian (or better Marxian) way as a system of needs, is distinguished from the state. It should be noted that the line of separation between the state of nature, the economic

sphere and civil society on the one hand, and the political
sphere and the state on the other, is always the line between
associations of equals (at least in the formal sense) and
associations of unequals.

Law and contract

The other conceptually and historically important distinction
which is involved in the great dichotomy is a distinction
between the sources (in the technical, legal sense of the
word) of public and private law: law and contract. Cicero
remarks that public law consists of *lex, senatus consultus*
and *foedus* (international treaty); private law consists of
the *tabulae*, the *pactum conventum* and the *stipulatio*
(*Partitiones oratoriae*, 37, 131). As can be seen, the criterion
for the distinction between public and private law are the
different ways in which they come into existence, both
being binding rules of conduct: public law is public in virtue
of being imposed by political authority and assumes the
specific form, increasingly prevalent with the passing of
time, of 'law' in the modern sense of the word; that is, of
a norm which is binding because it has been imposed by
the supreme power (sovereign) and is habitually enforced
through coercion (the exclusive use of which truly belongs
to the sovereign). Private law or, more precisely, the law
concerning private persons, represents the set of norms
established by individuals to regulate their reciprocal
relations, the most important of which are patrimonial
relations, through bilateral agreements whose force lies
primarily and independently of public regulation on the
principle of reciprocity (*do ut des*).

The explanatory force of the superimposition of the two
dichotomies private/public and law/contract is revealed in
the modern doctrine of natural law, where contract is the
typical form of how individuals govern their relations in
the state of nature (that is, in the state where a public
power does not as yet exist); whereas the law, usually

defined as the highest expression of the sovereign power (*voluntas superioris*), is the form in which the relations amongst subjects and between the state and subjects are regulated in civil society: that is, in a society which is held together by an authority that stands above individuals. The contrast of the state of nature and civil society as the contrast between the sphere of free contractual relations and the sphere of relations regulated by the law was taken over and strengthened by Kant, who brought to its conclusion the process of the identification of the two great dichotomies of legal doctrine: private law/public law on one side and natural law/positive law on the other; private law is the law that comes from the state of nature and its fundamental institutions are property and contract, whereas public law derives from the state and is constituted at the suppression of the state of nature and is, therefore, positive law in the proper sense of the word: a law whose binding force derives from the possibility that the coercive power of the state belonging exclusively to the sovereign will be exercised on its behalf.

The clearest confirmation of the fact that the contrast between private and public law passes through the distinction between contract and law comes from the criticism that the post-natural-law writers (above all, Hegel) make of natural law contractualism; that is, the doctrine which founds the state on the social contract. For Hegel, an institution of private law, such as contract, cannot be the legitimate foundation of the state for at least two reasons, closely connected to the very nature of contractual obligations as distinct from obligations that derive from law. In the first place the bonds that unite the state to its citizens are permanent and irrevocable, whereas the contractual bond can be revoked by the parties; and in the second place, because the state can demand from its citizens – even if only in exceptional circumstances – the sacrifice of the greatest good, life, which is (contractually speaking) unavailable. It is not by chance that every critic of natural law rejects contractualism as an essentially *private* and inadequate conception of the state which for Hegel draws its legitimacy, and therefore its right to command and be obeyed, either from the simple fact of representing the spirit of the people in a given situation, or from being the incarnation of the man of destiny (the 'hero' or 'man of *universal history*'), in both cases with a strength that transcends anything that might derive from the aggregation and agreements of individual wills.

Commutative justice and distributive justice

The third distinction which flows into the public/private dichotomy and which can both illuminate and be illuminated by it deals with the two classical forms of justice: distributive justice and commutative justice. Commutative justice governs exchange; its fundamental presumption is that in order for an exchange to be considered just, the two things exchanged must be of equal value. In a buying-and-selling transaction the right price corresponds to the value of the thing bought; in a work contract, the just wage corresponds to the quality or quantity of the work accomplished; in civil law, the indemnity which corresponds to the extent of damage is the just one; in penal law the just penalty occurs where there is a correspondence between the *malum actionis* and the *malum passionis*. The difference between these four typical cases is that in the first two the replacement of one good for another has taken place, whereas in the last two one evil substitutes another. Distributive justice is the principle guiding public authority in the distribution of honours and duties. Its claim is that everyone is given his due on the basis of criteria which can change according to the diversity of the objective situation or of the point of view: the most common criteria are 'to each according to his merit', 'to each according to his needs' and 'to each according to his work'. In other words, commutative justice is defined as that which takes place between the parts and distributive justice as that taking place between the whole and the parts. This new identification of the private sphere as the locus of commutative justice on the one hand and the public sphere as the locus of distributive justice on the other comes about through the mediation of the distinction already mentioned between associations of equals and associations of unequals. A clear example of such a mediation is given by Vico, for whom commutative justice, which he calls *equatrix*, governs an association of equals while distributive justice, called *rectrix*, governs an association of unequals, like the family and the state (1720, ch. LXIII).

Once again it is necessary to handle all these relationships with care because the coincidence of one with another is never perfect. In this instance as well, the limiting cases are the family and international society: the family is a private law institution in so far as it exists within the ambit of the state but it is at the same time an association of unequals and ruled by distributive justice; international society, which is, on the contrary, an association of equals (formally) and is governed by commutative justice is generally attributed to the public sphere, at least *ratione subiecti*, in that the subjects of international society, states, are public entities *par excellence*.

THE EVALUATIVE USE OF THE GREAT DICHOTOMY

Besides the descriptive meaning illustrated in the two preceding sections, the two terms of the public/private dichotomy also have an evaluative meaning. We are dealing with two terms which in descriptive use commonly function as contradictory terms, in the sense that in the universe defined by them no element can be both public and private simultaneously or even neither public nor private. Similarly, the evaluative meaning of one also tends to be opposed to the other in the sense that, when a positive evaluative meaning is attributed to one, the second acquires a negative evaluative meaning and vice versa. This derives from two different conceptions of the relations between public and private, the first of which can be defined as the primacy of the private over the public, and the second as the primacy of the public over the private.

The primacy of the private

The primacy of private law is affirmed in the diffusion and reception of Roman law in the Western world: the so-called law of the *Pandette* is for the most part private law, the principal institutions of which are the family, property, contracts and inheritance. In the length of its duration and the universality of its range Roman private law acquires the value of the law of reason; that is, of a law whose validity has come to be recognized independently of the circumstances of the time and place of its origin and is believed to be founded on the nature of things. This process is not very different from that when, many centuries later, the doctrine of the first economists, later called the classical economists (just like the great jurists of the golden age of Roman jurisprudence), was considered the only economics possible because it discovered, mirrored and described natural relations (that is, relations which were genuinely part of nature's domain, or 'physiocracy'). In other words, Roman private law, although originally historical and positive law (codified in the *Corpus iuris*), was transformed through centuries of work by jurists, annotators, commentators and systematizers into natural law, and then with the great codifications at the beginning of the nineteenth century, especially Napoleon's (1804), was transformed into positive law to which, however, its first commentators attributed an absolute validity, considering it as the law of reason.

For centuries, therefore, private law was law *par excellence*. In Hegel, *Recht* has still without any doubt the meaning of private law, the 'abstract law' of *The Philosophy of Right* (1821), while public law is given, at least in the first writings, the name of *Verfassung*, or constitution. Marx, too, when he spoke of law and developed the criticism (which today would be called ideological) of law always referred to private law whose principal institution is a contract between formally (if not substantively) equal elements. The law which Marx identified with bourgeois law is essentially private law, while the critique of public law is presented under the form of a critique of not so much a type of law but more a traditional conception of the state and political power. Pašukanis, the first and major theorist of Soviet law, will say (1924) that 'the most solid nucleus of the legal nebula lies in the field of the relations of private law', since the fundamental presupposition of legal regulation (and here 'private' should be added) is 'the antagonism of private interests' which explains why 'Roman legal thought has preserved its value until our times: it remains the *ratio scripta* of any society producing goods.' Finally, criticizing as ideological and unscientific the distinction between private and public law, Kelsen observed (1960) that the relations of private law can be defined 'as "legal relations" *tout court*, as relations "of law" in the strictest sense of the word, in order to contrast them with relations of public law as relations of "power".'

Public law as a systematic body of norms came into existence much later than private law: actually only in the era of the formation of the modern state, even if it is possible to find its origins in a fourteenth-century commentator such as Bartolo di Sassoferrato. However, while works of private law on property and possession and on contract and wills are exclusively legal treatises, the great treatises on the state, even when written by lawyers, from the *Six Livres de la République* by Bodin (1576) to Jellinek's *General Doctrine of the State* (*Allgemeine Staatslehre*) (1911) were never exclusively legal works. Not that Roman law had not furnished some authoritative principles for the solution of certain major problems of European public law beginning with the *lex regia de imperio* (*Digesto, 1, 4, 1*), according to which whatever the sovereign establishes has the force of law (*habet legis vigorem*) when the people have already attributed to their sovereign this power which originally belongs to the people: thus giving rise to the ancient dispute about whether the people have really transmitted or only conceded power to the sovereign. But with the dissolution of the ancient state and the formation of the German kingdoms, political relations underwent a transformation so profound, and in medieval society problems were so diverse (for example, the relations between church and state, between the Emperor and the kings, between the kings and the city), that Roman law could offer few instruments of interpretation and analysis. It still remains to be noted, however, that the two fundamental categories of European public law, used for centuries by jurists in the construction of a legal theory of the state, were derived from private law: the *dominium*, understood as the patrimonial power of the monarch over the territory of the state, and as such distinguished from the *imperium* which stands for the power of command over subjects; and the *pactum* in all its varieties (*societatis, subiectonis, unionis*) which functions as the principle of the legitimation of power in the contractualistic tradition that goes from Hobbes to Kant.

One of the events which best illustrates the persistent primacy of private over public law is the resistance that the law of property puts up against the sovereign's power to interfere and therefore to the sovereign's right to expropriate, for reasons of public utility, the goods of a subject. Even a theorist of absolutism like Bodin considered as unjust the sovereign who violated the property of subjects without a just and reasonable motive, seeing it as a violation of the natural law that ruled over all people equally, prince and commoner alike (1576, I, 8). Hobbes, who endowed the sovereign with unchecked power over the private lives of subjects, recognized that those subjects were free to do everything that the sovereign had not forbidden and the first example which occurs to him is the liberty to buy, sell and make other contracts amongst themselves (1651, ch. XXI). With Locke, property becomes a genuine natural right because it originates from personal effort in the state of nature before the constitution of political power, and therefore the free exercise of this right must be guaranteed by the law of the state (which is the law of the people). Through Locke, the inviolability of property (which included all other natural rights of the individual such as life and liberty, and which implies that there exists a sphere of autonomy different from the sphere of public power) became one of the cardinal points of the liberal conception of the state, which in this context can be defined as the most conscious, coherent and historically relevant theory of the primacy of the private over the public. The autonomy of the private sphere of the individual compared to the state's sphere of competence was taken over by Constant as the symbol of the liberty of the moderns compared to the ancients within the context of a philosophy of history in which the *esprit de commerce*, which motivates individual energies, is designed to supersede the *esprit de conquête* which motivates the holders of political power; the private sphere enlarges itself at the expense of the public sphere, if not to the point of eliminating the state then until its reduction to a minimum. Spencer celebrates this reduction by contrasting military societies of the past and industrial societies of the present understood as the contrast of a society where the public sphere prevails over the private and vice versa.

The primacy of the public

The primacy of the public has assumed different forms according to the various ways in which it has manifested itself but, above all in the last century, in the reaction to the liberal conception of the state and the historical if not definitive defeat of the minimalist state. It is founded on the contrast between collective and individual interests, on the necessary subordination and eventual suppression of the second by the first, as well as on the irreducibility of the common good to the sum of individual welfare and therefore on a criticism of one of the recurring theses of simple utilitarianism. It assumes various forms according to

the different ways in which the collective entity is understood – nation, class, the community of people – in whose
favour the individual must renounce his or her autonomy.
Not that all theories of the primacy of the public can be
put historically and politically on the same level, but
common to all is the idea that they boil down to the
following common principle: the whole comes before the
parts. We are dealing with an Aristotelian and later a
Hegelian idea (from a Hegel who explicitly cites Aristotle
in this matter), according to which the totality has ends
which cannot be reduced to the sum of the aims of the
individual members that compose it, and that, once the
good of the totality has been achieved, transforms itself
into the good of its parts; or to put it another way, the
greatest good of the subjects is the effect not of its pursuit
through personal effort and the antagonism of everyone's
interests, but of the contribution which each individual
together with the rest can collectively give to the common
good according to the rules which the whole community,
or the group which directs it (apparently or in reality),
imposes through its organs, be they autocratic or democratic.

Practically speaking, the primacy of the public means the
increase of state intervention in the coercive regulation
of individuals and sub-state groups, a reversal of the
emancipation of civil society from state interference which
was one of the historical consequences of the birth, growth
and hegemony of the bourgeois classes (civil society and
bourgeois society are the same thing in the Marxian
vocabulary and partially so in the Hegelian one). With the
collapse of limits to state action whose ethical foundations
were in the natural law tradition of the moral priority of
the individual over the group, and in the consequent
affirmation of the natural rights of the individual, the state,
little by little, reappropriated the space conquered by
bourgeois civil society to the extent of absorbing it
completely in the extreme example of the totalitarian state
(total in the sense that it does not leave any space outside
itself). Hegel's philosophy of law represents at the same

time both a belated awareness and an unconsciously advanced representation of this reabsorption of civil society by the state: it is a philosophy of law reflected in a philosophy of history which judges as decadent an epoch in which private law is dominant, such as the imperial Roman age, which moved between the two poles of public despotism and the liberty of private property, or such as the feudal age in which political relations are contractual and where, in fact, the state does not exist. As against this, progressive epochs are, according to Hegel, those in which public law takes revenge on private law: for example, the modern age, which is witness to the rise of the great territorial and bureaucratic state.

Two parallel processes

It has already been said above that the public/private distinction is duplicated in the politics/economics distinction with the consequence that the primacy of the public over the private has come to be interpreted as the primacy of politics over economics or, in other words, of the order directed from above over spontaneous order, of the vertical organization of society over its horizontal organization. Proof of this lies in the fact that the process, which up to now seemed irreversible, of the intervention of public powers in the regulation of the economy was also termed as the process of 'the publicization of the private'. It is a process which politically practical socialist doctrines have favoured, while the liberals of yesterday and today, not to mention the various strains of liberal socialism, have deprecated and continue to deprecate as one of the perverse products of mass society in which the individual, like the Hobbesian slave, requests protection in exchange for liberty; unlike the Hegelian slave destined to become free because engaged in the struggle not to save life but for personal recognition.

In fact, the publicization of the private is just one of two aspects of the evolution of the most industrially advanced societies. It is accompanied and complicated by an opposite process which can be called 'the privatization of the public' which is the reverse of what was foreseen by Hegel, according to whom the state as an ethical totality would end up by imposing itself on the fragmentation of civil society interpreted as an 'atomistic system'. The contractual relations characteristic of the world of private relations have not in fact been relegated to the lesser sphere of the relations between individuals or minor groups, but have re-emerged on the higher plane of politically important relations under at least two forms: in the relations between large trade union organizations for the formation and renewal of collective contracts, and in the relations between political parties for the formation of governmental coalitions. The life of a modern state in which civil society is constituted by increasingly strongly organized groups is criss-crossed by group conflicts which renew themselves continuously, in the face of which the state, together with the organs of decision (parliament and government) and of execution (the bureaucratic apparatus), takes on the role of mediator and guarantor more than the holder of imperial power according to the classical image of sovereignty. Agreements between trade unions and between parties are usually preceded by the long negotiations typical of contractual relations and finish in an agreement which is more like an international treaty, with the inevitable *rebus sic stantibus* clause, than a contract of private law for whose eventual dissolution the law establishes rules. Collective contracts concerning trade unions and governmental coalitions concerning political parties are decisive moments for the life of that great organization, or system of systems, the contemporary state, which is differentiated internally into semi-sovereign organizations among which are the large enterprises, trade union organizations and political parties. It is not by chance that those who look on the growth of these power centres as an attack on the sovereignty of the state speak of a new feudalism, understood really as the age in which, to speak as Hegel did, private law is pre-eminent over public law and this abuse of the superior by the inferior sphere highlights the ongoing process of the degeneration of the state.

Indeed, the two processes – the publicization of the private and the privatization of the public – are not incompatible and in fact interpenetrate each other. The first reflects the process of the subordination of private interests to collective interests represented by a state which increasingly surrounds and invades civil society; the second represents the revenge of private interests through the formation of large organized groups which make use of the public apparatus in order to achieve their own aims. The state can correctly be seen as the place where these conflicts occur and re-occur, settle down and flare up through the legal instrument of a continually remade agreement which is the modern equivalent of the traditional social contract.

THE SECOND MEANING OF THE DICHOTOMY

Public or secret

One should not confuse the public/private dichotomy that has been dealt with up to now with the distinctions whereby public means 'open to the public', 'performed in front of spectators', and private, in contrast, is that which is said or done in a restricted circle of people or, taken to the extreme, in secret. This distinction is also conceptually and historically relevant but within a conceptual system and historical context different from those in which the great dichotomy is placed; so different that the great dichotomy maintains its validity intact even when the public sphere, understood as the sphere of competence of political power, does not necessarily coincide with the sphere of the public, understood as the sphere where political power is controlled by the public. Conceptually and historically, the problem of the publicity of power is distinct from the problem of the nature of public power (public power, that is, contrasted with the power of private individuals). Political power is always public power in the meaning of the great dichotomy even when it is not public, does not act in public, is hidden from the public and is not controlled by the public. Conceptually, the problem of the publicity of power is always used to highlight the difference between two forms of government: the republic, characterized by public control of power and, in the modern age, the free formation of public opinion; and the monarchy, whose method of government includes recourse to the *arcana imperii*, that is to state secrecy, which in the modern constitutional state is allowed only as an exceptional remedy. Historically, the same problem marks out an epoch of profound transformation of the image of the state and of the relations between sovereign and subjects, the epoch of the birth of the 'political public' in Habermas's sense, where the public sphere acquires an institutional influence on government through the legislative body and acquires that influence because 'the exercise of public dominion has been effectively subjected to the democratic obligation of publicity' (1964).

Publicity and invisible power

The history of political power understood as power open to the public began with Kant, who considered the principle according to which 'all actions affecting the rights of other men are unjust if their maxim is not reconcilable with publicity' as the 'transcendental formula of public law' (1796). The meaning of this principle can be clarified by noting that there are maxims which, once made public, excite such a reaction that their implementation becomes impossible. What state could declare, when putting its signature to an international treaty, that it does not regard itself as bound by the norm that the pacts be observed? And even bearing in mind the all-too-common facts, what official could declare on assuming office that he or she will make use of it for personal gain, or to subsidize clandestinely a party, or to corrupt a judge who is hearing the case of one of the official's relations?

The principle of the publicity of the actions of those who wield public power (public here in the sense of political) is opposed to the theory of the *arcana imperii*, dominant in the age of absolute power. This theory states that the power of the prince is more effective and in keeping with its aim the more it is hidden from the indiscreet gaze of the populace, and the more (like God's) it is invisible. Two main arguments support this doctrine: one is intrinsic to the nature of the supreme power whose actions have more success the more rapid and unforeseeable they are: public control, even of an assembly of notables, slows down the decision and removes the element of surprise. The other argument is based on contempt for the public seen as a passive object, like a 'savage beast' that must be domesticated, dominated as it is by strong passions which prevent it from forming a rational opinion on the common good, short-sightedly egotistic and the ready prey of demagogues who use it for their own profit.

The invisibility and, consequently, the uncheckability, of power were assured, institutionally, by taking political decisions in a place not open to the public (the secret Cabinet) and by the non-publicity of those decisions and, psychologically, through the professed and recognized license to simulate and dissimulate: a principle of state action which breaks the moral law against lying. These two expedients, psychological and institutional, are complementary in the sense that they reinforce each other. The first allows sovereigns not to make known in advance which decisions they will take and not even to make them known once taken; the second allows them to hide the decision taken or to present it in a different manner. Naturally, where power is invisible so must counterpower also be invisible: as a consequence, the secrecy of the council chamber is checked by the palace conspiracy secretly hatched in the same places where sovereign power is hidden. Alongside the *arcana imperii* one always finds *arcana seditionis*.

While the principality in the classical sense of the word
– the monarchy of divine right and the various forms of
despotism – require and, in different ways, justify invisible
power, the democratic republic – *res publica*, not only in
the usual sense of the word but also in the sense of 'shown
to the public' – requires that power be visible. The place
where power is exercised in every form of republic is the
citizens' assembly (direct democracy), where the process of
decision-making resides by its very nature; for example,
the *agora* of the Greeks. Where the assembly is a meeting
of representatives of the people and consequently the
decision would be public for them alone and not all the
people, the meeting of the assembly must be open to the
public in such a manner that any citizen can have access
to it. There are some, like Carl Schmitt, who claim to have
found a link between the principle of representation and
the publicity of power, where 'representation can only take
place in the sphere of publicity' and 'no representation can
take place in secret and privately' so that 'a parliament has
a representative character only insofar as it is believed that
its activity is public' (1928). From this point of view the
exercise of various rights of freedom are essential to
democracy, allowing the formation of public opinion and
assuring that the actions of the rulers are drawn out of the
Cabinet room, flushed out from the hidden places to which
they attempt to flee from the public eye, examined, judged
and criticized when they are made known.

The process of the publicization of the private is
accompanied but never conclusively outflanked by the
inverse process of the privatization of the public, and so
the victory of visible over invisible power is never achieved
once and for all. Invisible power resists the advance of the
visible and is always inventing new ways of hiding itself
and of seeing without being seen. The ideal form of power
is the power attributed to God, the invisible all-seer. The
arcana imperii are transformed into state secrecy and, in a
modern constitutional state, take the concrete form of
punishing the publication of reserved acts and documents;

there is, however, this substantial difference: that as against the *arcanum*, seen as an essential instrument of power and therefore necessary, state secrecy is legitimate only in exceptional cases provided for by law. Similarly, the practice of concealment has never entirely disappeared because of the influence public power can exercise on the press, because of the monopolization of the means of mass communication, and above all because of the unscrupulous exercise of ideological power, the function of ideology being to veil the real motivations which act upon power (a public and legitimate form of the 'noble lie' of Platonic origin or of the 'permissible lie' of the theorists of *raison d'état*).

On the other hand, if it is true that in a democratic state power is more open to public scrutiny than in an autocratic state, it is also true that the use of computers (which are being used more and more to store the personal files of citizens) allows the holders of power to know more about the public than was possible in past states. The new prince can get to know far more about his subjects than most absolute monarchs of the past. Which goes to show that, notwithstanding the profound transformation of relations between rulers and ruled brought about by the development of democracy, the process of the publicization of power (and also in the second sense of the public/private dichotomy) is anything but linear. It remains the case that this dichotomy, whether in the sense of collective/individual (seen in the first three sections of this chapter) or in the sense of manifest/secret (as seen in this section), constitutes one of the fundamental and traditional categories, even with its changing meanings, for conceptual representation of historical comprehension and for the enunciation of value judgements, in the vast area covered by the theory of society and of the state.

2

Civil Society

In today's political vocabulary the term 'civil society' is generally used for one of the terms in the great dichotomy civil society/state, which means that it is impossible to fix its meaning and extension without doing the same for the term 'state'. By civil society is meant, negatively, the realm of social relations not regulated by the state: which is understood narrowly and nearly always polemically as the complex of apparatuses that exercise coercive power within an organized social system. The distinction between *societas civilis sine imperio* and *societas civilis cum imperio* goes back to August Ludwig von Schloezer (1794) and continually comes up in the German literature on the subject. The second expression stands for what is designated by the state in a context, as we shall see, where the contrast between state and society has not yet arisen and one term is enough to indicate either, albeit with an internal species-distinction. Occurring along with the restrictive notion of the state as an organ of coercive power and allowing the formation of, and accounts for, the persistence of the great dichotomy is the group of ideas that accompanies the birth of the bourgeois world: the affirmation of natural rights belonging to the individual and to social groups independently of the state and which limit and restrain political power; the discovery of a sphere of inter-individual relations – such as economic relations – whose regulation does not need the existence of coercive power because they are self-regulating;

the general idea so well expressed by Thomas Paine who was the author of a celebrated piece extolling the rights of man. He said that society is created by our needs and the state by our wickedness (1776) because humankind is naturally good and every society, in order to preserve itself and prosper, needs to limit the scope of civil laws that are imposed by coercion so as to allow the widest application of natural laws which do not need coercion in their application; in other words, the widening of private law with which individuals regulate their reciprocal relations guided by their real interests – of which everyone is *iudex in causa sua* – to the detriment of public and political law where the *imperium* is exercised which is understood as command by a superior who, as *iudex super partes*, has the right of exercising coercive power. It cannot be overemphasized that for the use of 'civil society', in the sense of the sphere of social as distinct from political relations, we are indebted to German writers (especially Marx and Hegel, as will be seen later) working in a language where *bürgerliche Gesellschaft* means both civil and bourgeois society; and that, in legal language which was fully asserting itself at the end of the eighteenth century, civil law as distinct from penal law included matters traditionally belonging to private law (the *Code civil* is the code of private law, *bürgerliches Recht* in German).

It is precisely because the expression 'civil society' in its eighteenth-century and contemporary meaning derives from the contrast which was unknown to tradition, between a political and a non-political sphere, that it is easier to come up with a negative rather than a positive definition: the more so because in treatises of public law and general doctrine of the state (the *allgemeine Staatslehre* of the German academic tradition from Georg Jellinek to Felix Ermacora) a positive definition of the state is never lacking. Civil society is the complex of relations not regulated by the state and consequently is the residue once the realm in which state power is exercised has been well defined. But even with such a vague notion it is possible to distinguish various emphases depending on whether the identification of the non-state with the pre-state, the anti-state or the post-state prevails. When one speaks of civil society in the first of these uses it means to say, whether in conscious or unconscious agreement with natural law doctrine, that before the state there were various forms of association formed by individuals among themselves for the satisfaction of their different interests and on which the state was imposed in order to regulate them but not to hamper their further development or prevent their continued renewal; one can talk in this case, although not in a strictly Marxist way, of civil society as an infrastructure and the state as a superstructure. In the second usage, civil society acquires a positive value connotation and indicates the place where all changes in the relations of domination manifest themselves, where groups form to fight for emancipation from political power and where so-called countervailing power gains strength. However, it is also possible to assign a negative value if the state's viewpoint is taken and the ferments of renewal of which civil society is the bearer are seen as the germs of disintegration. In the third usage, civil society has a meaning that is both chronological like the first and evaluative like the second: it represents the ideal of a society without a state which will spring from the dissolution of political power. This usage is present in the thought of Gramsci where the characteristic ideal of all Marxist thought on the extinction of the state is described as the 'reabsorption of political society into civil society' (1930–2a), as the civil society liberated from political society where hegemony, as opposed to domination, is practised. In the three different usages the non-state assumes three different guises: as the pre-condition of the state or, in other words, that which is not-yet-state in the first; as the antithesis of the state or else as that which poses as an alternative to the state in the second: and of the dissolution and end of the state in the third.

It is difficult to provide a positive definition of 'civil society' because it is a question of listing everything that has been left over after limiting the sphere of the state. It is enough to note that in many contexts the contrast between civil society and political institutions is a reformulation of the old contrast between real nation and legal nation. What is the real nation? What is civil society? As a first approximation we can say that civil society is the place where economic, social, ideological and religious conflicts originate and occur and that state institutions have the task of solving them either by mediating or preventing or repressing them. The agents of these conflicts and therefore of civil society proper, in so far as it is contrasted with the state, are social classes (or, more broadly, the groups, movements, associations and organizations that represent them or declare themselves their representatives); as well as class organizations there are interest groups, associations of various types with social and indirectly political ends, ethnic emancipation movements, civil rights groups, women's liberation, youth movements and so on. Parties have one foot in civil society and the other in institutions; so much so that it has been proposed to enrich the dichotomous conceptual scheme by inserting the concept of political society between the two concepts of civil society and state in order to encompass the phenomenon of parties which in reality do not entirely belong either in civil society or the state. In fact, one of the most frequent ways of defining political parties is to show that they perform the functions of selecting, aggregating and transmitting demands originating in civil society and which will become objects of political decision. In the most recent system-theories of society as a whole, civil society occupies the space reserved for the formation of demands (input) aimed at the political system and to which the political system has the task of supplying answers (output): the contrast between civil society and state therefore is posed as the contrast between the quantity and quality of demands and the capacity of institutions to give rapid and adequate answers.

The much-discussed contemporary problem of the governability of complex societies can also be interpreted in terms of the classic dichotomy between civil society and the state: a society becomes more ungovernable the greater the demands of civil society and the lack of a corresponding capacity of institutions to respond to them. In fact, the capacity of the state to respond may have reached absolute limits (hence the argument, for example, about 'fiscal crisis'). The question of legitimacy is closely linked to the theme of ungovernability: ungovernability generates the crisis of legitimacy. This question can also be translated into the dichotomy's terms. Institutions represent legitimate power in the Weberian sense of the word: that is, power whose decisions are accepted and realized in so far as they emanate from an authority recognized as having the right to make binding decisions for the whole collectivity. Civil society is the place where, especially in periods of institutional crisis, *de facto* powers are formed that aim at obtaining their own legitimacy even at the expense of legitimate power; where, in other words, the processes of delegitimation and relegitimation take place. This forms the basis of the frequent assertion that the solution of a grave crisis threatening the survival of a political system must be sought first and foremost in civil society where it is possible to find new sources of legitimation and therefore new sources of consensus. Finally, the sphere of civil society is generally taken to include the phenomenon of public opinion (understood as the public expression of agreement or dissent concerning institutions) which circulates through the press, radio, television and so on. Moreover, public opinion and social movements develop together and influence each other. Without public opinion – meaning, more concretely, without the channels of transmission of public opinion which becomes 'public' in so far as it is transmitted to the public – the sphere of civil society loses its typical function and disappears. At the extreme, the totalitarian state, which is a state that has entirely absorbed civil society, is a state without public opinion (that is, with only official opinion).

THE MARXIAN INTERPRETATION

The actual use of the expression 'civil society' as a term indissolubly linked to the state or political system, is of Marxian and, before Marx, Hegelian origin even if, as shall be seen, the Marxian use is more reductive than Hegel's. The frequency with which the expression 'civil society' is used even in everyday language is a result of the influence of Marxist literature on contemporary Italian political debate. Proof of this lies in the fact that in other linguistic contexts the expression 'civil society' is replaced in the same dichotomy by the term 'society': in Germany, for example, a full and learned debate has recently taken place on *Staat und Gesellschaft* (cf. Böckenförde 1976), where the term *Gesellschaft*, society, includes everything we mean by 'civil society'. The traditional *locus classicus* for the origin of the meaning of 'civil society' is Marx's preface to *A Critique of Political Economy* (1859), where he writes that through studying Hegel he arrived at the conclusion that legal and political institutions have their roots in the material relations of existence, 'the complex of which were embraced by Hegel under the term "civil society"', and he derived the consequence that 'the anatomy of civil society was to be found in political economy.' It does not matter that in this passage Marx gives a reductive and ultimately distorted view of Hegel's concept of 'civil society' as we shall see shortly; it is important to highlight that to the extent Marx makes civil society the site of economic relations, or rather the relations that constitute 'the real base on which a legal and political superstructure is elevated', 'civil society' comes to mean the complex of inter-individual relations that are outside or antecedent to the state: the same pre-state sphere which natural law writers and, to some extent in their wake, the first economists starting with the physiocrats, called the state of nature or natural society. The eventual substitution in Marxian language of the expression 'civil society' for 'natural society' is evidenced in a passage from an early work, *The Holy Family* (Marx and Engels 1845), where one reads: 'The modern State has civil society as a *natural base* (repeat, "natural"), the man of civil society, that is independent man, is united to other men through private interest and *unconscious* natural necessity.' Even more surprising is the fact that the specific character of civil society so defined coincides at every point with Hobbes's state of nature which, as is well known, is the war of all against all: 'All of *civil society* is really this war [of man against man], one against the other of every individual each isolated from the other by their *individuality* and it is the general, unrestrained movement of the elemental powers of life freed from the chains of privilege' (ibid.). This is surprising because in the natural law tradition (cf. 4) 'civil society' is what today would be called the state, the antithesis of the state of nature.

This transposition of the traditional meaning of the expression 'the state of nature' to meaning the expression to which it is traditionally contrasted, civil society, could not be explained without taking account once again that Marx's civil society is the *bürgerliche Gesellschaft* which, especially after Hegel and the interpretation of Hegel's texts by the Left Hegelians, acquired the meaning of 'bourgeois society' in the sense of class society, and that bourgeois society in Marx has the bourgeoisie as a historical subject, a class that achieved its political emancipation by liberating itself from the shackles of the absolute state and by opposing to the traditional state the rights of humankind and citizens which are in reality the rights that must, from then on, protect their particular class interests. A passage from the early *The Jewish Problem* (1843) makes clearer than any argument the transformation of the picture of the hypothetical state of nature into the historic reality of bourgeois society: 'Political emancipation at one time meant the emancipation of bourgeois society [which in this context could not translate meaningfully as 'civil'], from politics, from even the appearance of a universal content. Feudal society was dissolved into its fundamental element, man.

But the man that constituted that foundation was egoistic man.' The state of nature of natural law and Marx's bourgeois society share 'egoistic man' as a subject. And from egoistic man only an anarchic – or despotic – society can be born.

Notwithstanding the dominant influence of the Marxist notion of 'civil society' on the use of the expression, it cannot be said that the use has been consistent even within the Marxist tradition. The importance of the dichotomy between civil society and the state in Gramsci's thought has often been recognized. It would be wrong to believe, as many do, that Gramsci's dichotomy faithfully reproduces Marx's. While in Marx the moment of civil society concides with the material base (as opposed to the superstructure of ideologies and institutions), for Gramsci the moment of civil society is itself superstructural. In his notes on the intellectuals one reads: 'It is possible now to determine two important superstructural "levels": one which can be called "civil society", that is the group of organisms popularly called "private", and the other "political society or State"; they correspond to the functions of "hegemony" which the dominant group exercises throughout society and "direct domination" which manifests itself in the State and "legal" government' (1932).

To clarify this definition it is useful to bear in mind the historical example used by Gramsci when contrasting hegemony with direct domination: the example of the Catholic Church, understood as 'the apparatus of hegemony of the ruling group, which did not have its own apparatus, that is, did not have its own cultural and intellectual organization but felt the universal ecclesiastical organisation to be as such' (1930–2b). Gramsci, like Marx, considers ideologies part of the superstructure; but whereas Marx saw civil society as the complex of economic relations constituting the material base, Gramsci saw civil society as the sphere where ideological apparatuses operate and whose task it is to exercise hegemony and through hegemony to obtain consensus. It is not the case that Gramsci abandons the base/superstructure dichotomy and replaces it with the civil society/state dichotomy. He adds the second to the first, thereby making his conceptual scheme more complex. In order to represent the contrast between the structural moment and the superstructural moment he regularly makes use of these pairs: economic moment/political–ethical moment, necessity/liberty, objectivity/subjectivity. To represent the contrast between civil society and the state he uses other pairs: consensus/force, persuasion/coercion, morality/politics, hegemony/dictatorship, leadership/domination. It should be noted that in the first dichotomy the economic moment is contrasted with the political–ethical moment. Yet the second dichotomy can be considered as the resolution of the duality implicit in the second moment of the first: civil society represents the moment of 'morality' through which the dominant class obtains consensus and acquires legitimacy, to employ a modern expression not used by Gramsci; the state represents the political moment, strictly speaking, and exercises the force that is no less necessary than consensus for the maintenance of power: at least as long as power is exercised by a restricted and not a universal class (which exercises it through its party, the true protagonist of hegemony). It can be observed, at this stage, that Gramsci has unwittingly recovered the natural law meaning of civil society as a society founded on consensus. However, there is this difference: according to natural law, where the legitimacy of power depends on its being grounded on the social contract, the society of consensus *par excellence* is the state, while according to Gramsci the society of consensus is what will rise out of the extinction of the state.

THE HEGELIAN SYSTEM

When Marx writes that he had arrived at the discovery of civil society underlying political institutions through studying Hegel and identifies civil society with the sphere of economic relations, he is giving a partial interpretation of the Hegelian category of civil society and passing it on to the entire Hegelian–Marxist tradition. The Hegelian category of civil society, whose clear formulation and denomination Hegel only arrived at in the last stages of his thought (*Outlines of the Philosophy of Law*, 1821) is very much more complex and, on account of this, much more difficult to interpret. As an intermediate moment of ethicity, situated between the family and the state, it allows the construction of a triadic scheme which can be contrasted with two preceding dyadic models: the Aristotelian, based on the dichotomy between family and state (*societas domestica/societas civilis*, where *civilis*, from *civitas*, corresponds exactly to *politikós*, from *polis*) and the natural law model based on the dichotomy of state of nature/civil society. Compared to the family it is already an incomplete form of state, the 'state of the *intellect*'; compared to the state, it is not yet the state in its essence and in its full historical realization. In the Berlin lectures, civil society is divided into three moments: the system of needs, the administration of justice and the police (together with the corporation): the area of economic relations is covered only by the first while the second and the third moments include parts of the traditional doctrine of the state.

Looking for the anatomy of Hegel's civil society in political economy is partial and wayward in relation to a true understanding of Hegel's thought. What exactly Hegel's true thoughts might have been about the division of civil society is controversial: some believe that it was conceived as a kind of residual category and after many attempts, lasting 20 years, to systematize the traditional material of practical philosophy, Hegel ended up by placing there everything that he could not fit into the well-defined categories of the family and the state. The greatest difficulty with this interpretation lies in the fact that the larger part of the section is not dedicated to an analysis of political economy but to two important items in the doctrine of the state regarding respectively – to use contemporary

vocabulary – the judicial and the administrative functions
(under the name then current of police state). How could
Hegel, who was concluding his dissection of ethicity in the
state, precede it with a section in which he deals with two
areas of such importance for the delineation of the state as a
whole as the administration of justice and the administrative
state? Hegel's division, although continuing to be difficult
to render intelligible in the light of preceding and succeeding
traditions, can be understood, or at least made less singular,
if we bear in mind that in German *societas civilis* becomes
bürgerliche Gesellschaft which for centuries (and certainly
until Hegel) meant the state in contrast to the family in
the Aristotelian tradition and to the state of nature in the
natural law tradition. What differentiates Hegel's civil
society from its predecessors is not its retreat towards pre-
state society – a retreat that only comes with Marx – so
much as its identification as an imperfect state-form. Instead
of being, as some have interpreted, the moment *preceding*
the formation of the state, Hegel's civil society represents
the first stage of the formation of the state – the
legal–administrative state with the task of regulating external
relations while the state, strictly speaking, represents the
ethical/political moment whose job is to realize the inward
adhesion of citizens to the whole of which they are a part
– to the extent that the state can be called internal or
interior (Gentile's state *in interiore homine*). The Hegelian
distinction between civil society and the state, rather than
being a sequence in the pre-state and state forms of ethicity,
represents the distinction between an inferior and a superior
state. While the superior state is characterized by a
constitution and constitutional powers (monarchical power,
legislative power and governmental power), the lesser state
works through two subordinate legal powers: judicial power
and administrative power. The mainly negative job of the
first is to settle conflicts of interest and repress offences
against established law; of the second, to provide for the
common interest, intervening in the supervision of morals,
the distribution of work, education, the care of the poor:

that is, in all the activities that distinguish the *Wohlfahrt-Staat*, the state that looks after the external well-being of its subjects.

It can be further shown that going back to the traditional *societas civilis* for a clearer understanding of Hegel's civil society is not arbitrary from the meaning that this moment has in the development of Objective Spirit in the Hegelian system. Hegelian categories always have a historical dimension as well as a systematic role: they are at the same time interconnected parts of a global conception of reality and historical figures. Think of the state of law (*Rechtszustand*) of the *Phenomenology of Spirit* (*Phaenomenologie des Geistes*, 1807) which represents conceptually the condition where relations of private law are exalted and which is, historically, the Roman empire. Moreover, that civil society is a historical figure in Hegel's system was more than once confirmed by him when he said that ancient states – whether the despotic ones of the static Orient or the Greek cities – did not possess civil societies and that the 'discovery of civil society belongs to the modern world' (1821). For Hegel the error of those who had discovered civil society – and in this rebuke lies the argumentative significance of the location of this figure, not at the end of the process of Objective Spirit but in a position subordinate to the state in its entirety – lies in having believed that it exhausted the essence of the state. Therefore, civil society is not just a lesser form of the state in the complex of the system, but it also represents the concept of the state at which preceding political writers and jurists of public law had stopped, which can be called privatistic in the sense that its principal task is to settle conflicts of interest which have their origins in private relations by means of the administration of justice and subsequently to take care of the well-being of citizens by protecting them from the damage that comes from giving free rein to the egoistic particularism of individuals.

Behind this vision of civil society, which is narrow compared to a fully-developed state, it is possible to see an allusion to either Locke's theory of the state whose sole *raison d'être* is to prevent the private justice of the state of nature where there is no uninvolved and impartial judge and to protect property, understood as a natural right; or the eudemonistic state of the supporters of enlightened absolutism which also takes on the job of providing for the well-being of its subjects but which never rises above an individualist conception of social relations. Hegel was not ignorant of the fact that the eudemonistic state had already been criticized by Kant who, however, rejected it in the name of the state of law whose scope of action was limited to the guarantee of individual liberty in a manner that followed Locke's and did not anticipate the organic conception that alone could raise the state to the sphere of ethicity. Finally, the reason why Hegel placed his concept of the state above the concept at which his predecessors stopped must be sought in the necessity of explaining why the right of the state is recognized to request of citizens the sacrifice of their goods (through taxation) and of their lives (when it declares war); an explanation it is useless to seek in the contractualistic doctrine, where the state is born of an agreement which the contractors can dissolve when they like, or in the eudemonistic doctrine, where the supreme aim of the state is the well-being of its subjects. In the last instance what characterizes the state compared to civil society are the relations that the state alone and not civil society undertakes with other states so that it is true that the state and not civil society is the subject of universal history which concludes the development of Objective Spirit.

THE NATURAL LAW TRADITION

Hegel's use of civil society for the state, even if only an inferior form of state, corresponds to the traditional meaning of *societas civilis* where *civilis* from *civitas* is synonymous with *politikós* from *polis* and is an exact translation of the expression *koinonía politiké*. Aristotle uses it at the beginning of the *Politics* to indicate the *polis* or city whose character as an independent and self-sufficient community based on a constitution (*politeia*) was considered for centuries as the origin or historical precedent of the state in the modern sense of the word, even with two different meanings, depending on whether it is contrasted on the basis of the Aristotelian model, according to which the state is the natural successor to family society, to domestic or family society, or on the basis of the Hobbesian model (or natural law), for which the state is the anthithesis of the state of nature, to the *societas naturalis* constituted by hypothetically free and equal individuals. The difference lies in the fact that while the *societas civilis* of the Aristotelian model is still a natural society – in the sense that it corresponds perfectly to humankind's social nature (*politikòn zôon*) – the same *societas civilis*, in Hobbes's model (in so far as it is the antithesis of the state of nature and is constituted through the agreement of individuals who decide to get out of the state of nature), is an instituted or artificial society (*homo artificialis* or *machina machinarum*).

Nothing proves better the vitality and longevity of this expression than its consistent use in other contexts in which the opposite term is the family and contexts where the opposite term is the state of nature. The first usage one finds in Bodin, a typical representative of the Aristotelian tradition for whom the state is a natural fact: 'The State [*république* or *res publica*] is the civil society that can exist on its own without associations and other bodies, but it cannot do so without the family' (1576, III, 7). For the second take Kant, another authoritative and representative example of the natural law model: 'Man must leave the state of nature, in which everyone follows the caprices of his own imagination and unite with all others . . . submitting himself to an external and publicly legal constraint . . .: which is to say that everyone must, above all else, enter into a civil state' (1797). However through the persistence of the natural law model in the modern age, from Hobbes

to Kant, the contrasting of civil society to natural society
ended up making the expression 'civil society' mean
prevalently 'artificial society', so much so that a traditional
author like Haller, who sees the state along the lines of
the Aristotelian model as a natural society on a level with
the family – 'the highest rank of natural or private society'
(1816) – claims that 'the distinction, always reproduced in
currently accepted texts of doctrine, between civil society
and other natural societies, is without foundation', so that
'it is desirable that the expression *civil society* (*societas
civilis*) that has crept into our language from the Romans
should be entirely banned as soon as possible' (Haller
1816). An assertion of this kind cannot be explained unless,
through the natural law use of 'civil society', the expression
has assumed the exclusive meaning of state as an entity
instituted by people on top of natural relations, even as
the voluntary regulation of natural relations, in short as an
artificial society, while in its original Aristotelian meaning,
civil society, *koinonía politiké*, is a natural society on a
level with the family. In reality, what Haller wanted to
abandon was not so much the word but the meaning the
word took on for those, like natural lawyers, who saw
states (to use Haller's own polemical expression) as
'arbitrarily formed associations, distinct from all others by
virtue of their origins and their aims' (Haller 1816).

The expression 'civil society', still with the meaning of
political state as distinct from every form of non-political
state, was commonly adopted to distinguish the area of
competence of the state or civil power from the area of
competence of church or religious power, in the dichotomy
civil society/religious society which is added to the traditional
domestic society/civil society. Unknown to classical
antiquity, the distinction is a recurring one in Christian
thought. Take a Catholic writer like Antonio Rosmini-
Serbati. In the *Philosophy of Law*, the part dedicated to
social law examines three types of association necessary to
the 'perfect organisation of human kind' (1841–3). These
three associations are: religious or theocratic society,

domestic society and civil society. This tripartite division obviously derives from combining the dichotomy family/ state, which is the point of departure of the Aristotelian model, with the dichotomy church/state which is fundamental in the tradition of Christian thought.

The two meanings of 'civil society' as political society or state – and as such a society distinct from religious society – are enshrined in two articles of the *Encyclopédie* dedicated respectively to *Société civile* (Anon. 1765b) and to *Société* (1765a). In the first one comes across this definition: 'civil society means the political body that men of the same nation, the same state, of the same town or other place, form together, and the political links that attaches one to the others' (1765b). The second is dedicated almost exclusively to the problem of the relations between civil society and religious society with the aim of rigorously determining their respective spheres of influence.

CIVIL SOCIETY AS CIVILIZED SOCIETY

A much-repeated contemporary opinion on Hegel's intellectual sources claims that the notion of *bürgerliche Gesellschaft* was inspired by Adam Ferguson's *Essay on the History of Civil Society* (1767) which was translated into German in 1768 by Christian Garve and which Hegel certainly knew. However, it is one thing to claim that Ferguson (together with Adam Smith) might have been one of Hegel's sources as regards the section on civil society that deals with the system of needs and, more generally, political economy and another, on the basis of comparisons between Hegel's and Ferguson's texts, to say that the *bürgerliche Gesellschaft* of the latter has anything to do with the civil society of the former. Just because Hegel may have taken some pointers from Ferguson for dealing with some elements of political economy that form part of the analysis of civil society does not mean to say that the civil society in Ferguson has the same meaning as in Hegel. In fact civil society has a different meaning for Ferguson and the other Scots: *civilis* is no longer the adjective of *civitas* but of *civilitas*. Civil society also means civilized society (Smith, in fact, will use the term civilized) and has a near synonym in 'polished'. Ferguson's work, which describes the passage from primitive to evolved society, is a history of progress: humanity has passed and continues to pass from the savage condition of hunter peoples without property and without a state to the barbaric condition of people that take to agriculture and introduce the first germs of property, to a civilized condition characterized by the institution of property, by exchange and by the state. It cannot at all be excluded that in both the *societas civilis* of the natural lawyers and *bürgerliche Gesellschaft* is hidden civil society in Ferguson's and the Scots' meaning: it is sufficient to think of Hobbes's famous contrast between the state of nature and civil society, where *barbaries* appear among the characteristics of the first and *elegantia* of the second (1642, X, I), or of Hegel's repeated assertion that ancient states, whether despotic or Greek republic, did not have a civil society (a formation characteristic of the modern age). But it is still the case that Ferguson's civil society is civil not because it is different from domestic or natural society, but because it is in contrast to primitive society.

It is only by taking account of this meaning that one can fully understand Rousseau's *société civile*. In the *Discourse on the Origin and Grounds of Inequality among Men* (1754) Rousseau describes first of all the state of nature, the condition of natural man who does not yet live in society because it is not necessary to him since bountiful nature provides him with the satisfaction of his essential needs, and because he is happy in this condition; next he describes the state of corruption into which natural man falls following on the institution of private property that stimulates, exacerbates and perverts egoistic instincts, and on the invention of agriculture and metallurgy (that which today one would call techniques for increasing his power over nature which become transformed into instruments of the domination of man over man by the more able and the stronger). Rousseau called the state of corruption *société civile* where the adjective *civile* clearly means 'civilized', even though with a negative connotation that distinguishes his position on 'civility' from the majority of the writers of his time and in general from the Enlightenment ideology of progress. However, just as it is the majority of writers for whom civil society has principally the meaning of political society and the meaning of civilized society is not excluded, so in Rousseau the prevalent meaning of civil society as civilized society does not exclude that this society might be a political society in embryo unlike the state of nature – although in the corrupt form of the domination of the weak by the strong, the poor by the rich, the cunning over the simple-minded – a form of political society which man must leave in order to establish a republic based on the social contract: that is, on the unanimous agreement of each with all: just as in the natural law hypothesis, which starts from a reversed judgement of the two terms, man must leave the state of nature.

THE CURRENT DEBATE

This historical excursus has shown the variety of the often contrasting meanings for which the expression 'civil society' has been used. Summing up, the prevalent meaning was that of a political society or state used, however, in different contexts depending on whether civil or political society was distinguished from domestic society, natural society or religious society. Along with this the other tradition-al meaning that appears in the sequence savage society–barbarism–civilization which, starting with the writers of the eighteenth century, constitutes a classical scheme for outlining human progress (with the exception of Rousseau for whom civil society, although having the mean-ing of civilized society, represents a negative moment in historic development). A completely different story starts

with Hegel for whom for the first time civil society no
longer includes the state in its entirety but represents a
moment in the process of the formation of the state. He is
followed by Marx who, concentrating his attention on the
system of needs which constitutes only the first moment of
Hegel's civil society, includes in the sphere of civil
society exclusively material and economic relations, thereby
accomplishing an almost complete inversion of the traditional meaning, and not only separates civil society from
the state but makes it both its antithetical and foundational
moment. Finally Gramsci, although maintaining the distinction between civil society and the state, moved the former
from the sphere of the material base to the superstructure
and made it the locus of formation of ideological power,
as distinct from political power strictly understood, and of
the process of the legitimation of the ruling class.

In the current debate, as was said at the beginning, the
contrast remains. The idea that civil society is the antecedent
(or antithesis) of the state has so entered into everyday
practice that it now takes an effort to convince oneself that
for centuries the same expression was used to designate
that collection of institutions which, as a rule, today
constitute the state and which nobody would call civil society
without running the risk of a complete misunderstanding.
Naturally this has not occurred by chance or on account of
the whims of political writers. One should not forget that
societas civilis translates Aristotle's *koinonía politiké,* an
expression that designates the city as a form of community
different from and superior to the family, an organization
of living together having the characteristics of self-sufficiency
and independence which will later be characteristics of the
state in all its historical forms but which was not distinguished
or was never knowingly distinct from underlying economic
society, economic activity being an attribute of the family
(whence the name of economic for the management of the
house). That the state might be defined as a form of
society could be considered correct during the centuries of
controversy between state and church about the determi-

nation of their respective borders, a controversy that was seen from both sides as a conflict between the two societies, the *societas civium* and the *societas fidelium*; and not at all inappropriately when in the natural law doctrine and contractualism the state was seen above all as a voluntary association in defence of some pre-eminent interests such as the defence of life, property or liberty. It is not to be excluded that the traditional identification of the state as a form of society might have contributed to delaying the perception of the distinction between the social system as a whole and the political institutions through which domination is exercised (*Herrschaft* in the Weberian sense); a distinction that has been accentuated in the modern age with the development of economic relations beyond household management, on the one hand, and the development of the apparatus of public power on the other.

However, starting with Machiavelli – and this is one reason for considering him one of the founders of modern political science – the state can no longer in any way be assimilated to a form of society, and only for scholastic reasons can it still be defined as *societas civilis*. When Machiavelli spoke of the state he meant to speak of the greatest power that can be exercised over the inhabitants of a given territory and of the apparatus which certain individuals and groups use in order to acquire and maintain this power. The state thus understood is not the society state but the machine state. After Machiavelli, the state can still be defined as *societas civilis*, but the definition appears more and more incongruous and wayward. The contrast between society and the state which starts with the birth of bourgeois society is the natural consequence of a differentiation that occurred in things and, together with a conscious and increasingly necessary division of tasks, between those who occupy themselves with the 'wealth of nations' and those who deal with the political institutions, between political economy originally and then sociology on the one hand, and the science of the state and all its related disciplines, the *Polizeiwissenschaft*, statistics (in the original sense of the term), the science of administration and so on, on the other.

In the last few years the question has been asked whether the distinction between civil society and state that has lasted for two centuries still possesses a *raison d'être*. It has been said that the process of the emancipation of society from the state has been followed by the reverse process of the reappropriation of society by the state, that the state in transforming itself from the *Rechtsstaat* (constitutional state) into the social state (to use the term popularized above all by German lawyers and political scientists) is badly distinguished precisely because it is social from the underlying society that it pervades particularly through the regulation of economic relations. However, it has been noted that, along with the process of the state's colonization of society, there has been a reverse but no less significant process of society's colonization of the state through the development of the various forms of participation in political choice, the growth of mass organizations that directly or indirectly exercise political power: so that the expression 'social state' can be understood not only in the sense of a state that has permeated society but also in the sense of a state that has been permeated by society.

These remarks are correct and yet the contrast between civil society and state is still used: a sign that it reflects a real situation. Starting from the consideration that the two processes of the state-making-society and society-making-state are contradictory, because the completion of the first would lead to a state without society – the totalitarian state – and the accomplishment of the second to society without the state – the extinction of the state – the two processes are anything but accomplished, and are unaccomplishable simply because of their cohabitation and contradictoriness. These two processes are well represented by the two images of the participating citizen and the protected citizen, who are in conflict among themselves, sometimes in the same person: the citizen who through active participation always asks for greater protection from the state and through the request for protection strengthens the state which the citizen wants to control but which ends up becoming his or her master. Under this aspect society and state act as two necessary moments, separate but contiguous, distinct but interdependent, internal articulations of the social system as a whole.

3

State, Power and Government

Towards the study of the state

Historical disciplines

The two principal sources for the study of the state are the history of political institutions and the history of political doctrine. The fact that the history of institutions can be traced in terms of the history of doctrines should not allow the two kinds of history to be confused. The history of European parliaments is one thing, the history of writers on parliaments quite another. There is no doubt as to the importance of Aristotle's political works for the study of institutions in the Greek cities, or of the importance of the Sixth Book of Polybius' *Histories* for the study of the constitution of republican Rome. But nobody wishing to acquire a knowledge of the structure of the first large territorial states of the modern age would read Hobbes, and neither would they read Rousseau to learn about the structure of modern democracies. On the other hand, if the study of the works of Aristotle and the histories of Polybius is important both for a knowledge of the Greek cities and of the Roman republic, then other sources, literary or otherwise, from ancient to modern times, are required for a thorough knowledge of the mechanism through which power relations in a political system are instituted or modified. For obvious reasons, but essentially due to the difficulty of the availability of sources, the history of institutions developed later than the history of doctrines. Thus the structure of a given political system is known through the reconstruction and sometimes the idealization or distortion of those who have written about them. Hobbes has been identified with the absolute state, Locke with parliamentary monarchy, Montesquieu with the limited state, Rousseau with democracy, Hegel with constitutional monarchy and so on. The first source for the study of institutions, independent of doctrines, is constituted by historians: Machiavelli reconstructs the history and structure of the institutions of the Roman republic by commenting on Livy. Vico, in order to reconstruct the civil history of nations from their savage origins until the great states of his time, denounces the haughtiness of scholars who 'would like what they know to be as old as the world itself' (1744) and for his own research intends to 'give an account as if there had never been books in the world' (Vico 1744).

After the historical studies came the study of the laws which regulate relations between the ruled and the rulers: the complex of norms that make up public law (itself a doctrinal category). The first histories of institutions were histories of law written by jurists who often had direct practical experience of affairs of state. Today, the history of institutions is not only free of doctrinal theory, but has enlarged the study of civil structures beyond the legal forms which shape them. It includes a concrete analysis of the functioning of a particular institution during a given period using written documents as well as the testimony of authors and the opinions of contemporaries. These proceed from the study of a fundamental institution (such as parliament and its fate in other countries) to the study of particular institutions (such as the office of secretary of state, superintendent or the secret Cabinet). In this way the passage of the feudal state to absolute monarchy, or the gradual formation of the administrative apparatus and hence of the contemporary state, can be traced.

Philosophy and political science

The state, apart from its historical development, comes to be studied both as a complex system in itself – its structures, functions, constitutive elements, mechanisms, organs and so on – and in its relations with contiguous systems. Today, this immense field of study is conventionally divided between two disciplines which are didactically distinct: political philosophy and political science. Like all artificial distinctions, this one is both tenuous and questionable. When Hobbes called the sum of analyses of humankind in their social relations *philosophia civilis* he was including a series of matters which today would belong to political science; Hegel, on the other hand, gave to his *Outline of a Philosophy of Right* (1821) the subtitle of *Staatswissenschaft im Grundrisse (Outline of a Science of the State)*. Political philosophy involves three types of research. These are: (a) the best form of government or the best republic; (b) the foundations of the state or political power, with the consequent justification or denial of political obligation; and (c) the essence of the political ('politicalness') and the important dispute on the distinction between ethics and politics. These three forms of political philosophy are perfectly represented at the beginning of the modern age by three works which have left indelible marks on the history of political thought. More's *Utopia* (1516) offered a blueprint of the ideal republic. Hobbes's *Leviathan* (1651) claimed to give a rational, and therefore universal, justification for the existence of the state as well as providing reasons why its commands should be obeyed. Machiavelli's *The Prince* (1513), which, at least according to one interpretation, is the only one to give rise to an '-ism' (Machiavellianism), identifies the specific character of political action and how it can be distinguished from moral action.

By political science is meant research into that area of political life which satisfies three conditions: (a) the principle of verification or falsification as a criterion of the acceptability of its results; (b) the use of scientific techniques which allow a strong or weak causal explanation of the phenomenon investigated; (c) an absence of, or abstention from, value judgements ('value freedom'). Looking at these three forms of political philosophy described above, we can see how each one lacks at least one of the characteristics of science. Political philosophy, as research into the best form of republic, does not have a value-free character. As research into the ultimate foundations of power it does not mean to explain the phenomenon of power but to justify it, an operation which has as its aim the characterization of behaviour as either permitted or forbidden. This cannot be done without recourse to values. As an investigation into the essence of politics it withdraws from any empirical verification or falsification, because what is presumptuously called 'the essence of politics' derives from a nominal definition and as such is neither true nor false.

Legal and sociological perspectives

The theme of the state can be approached from points of view other than those conventionally entitled 'political philosophy' and 'political science'. For a long time after Georg Jellinek wrote his *General Doctrine of the State* (1911), the distinction between sociological and legal doctrines became necessary after public law became technical and the characterization of the state as a legal person which resulted from it. The fact that public law became technical was, in its turn, the natural consequence of the conception of state as a *'Rechtsstaat'*, as a state conceived primarily as a legally-produced entity and in general as a legal structure. This reconstruction of the state as a legal structure, however, should not allow us to forget that the state, through law, is also a form of social organization and as such cannot be dissociated from society and from underlying social relations. The necessity then arises of distinguishing between the legal perspective (the prerogative of lawyers, who for centuries had been the principal writers of treatises on the state), and the sociological perspective (which makes use of the contributions of sociologists, ethnologists and students of various forms of social organization), a distinction which could not have occurred before the arrival on the scene of sociology as a general theory incorporating a theory of the state.

It was Weber who recognized the importance of Jellinek's distinction and who, taking a hint from the *General Doctrine of the State*, maintained the need to distinguish between legal and sociological perspectives. Jellinek had stated that the social doctrine of the state 'had for its content the objective, historical or natural existence of the State', whereas legal doctrine was concerned with 'legal norms which in that real existence must manifest themselves' (1911) and founded the distinction on the opposition – destined to find favour – between the spheres of the 'is' and the 'ought'. Weber, now considered one of the founders of the sociological approach to jurisprudence, stated that 'when we speak of law, legal order and legal norms, it is necessary to separate rigorously the legal point of view from the sociological' (Weber 1908–20): a distinction which he rooted in the difference between ideal validity, with which jurists are concerned, and empirical validity, with which sociologists are concerned. For Weber, this was an indispensable premise in order to make it clear that he would be concerned with the state of the sociologist and not the jurist. This approach becomes a chapter in the development of the theory of social groups of which one type is the political group which in their turn become states (that is, a modern state) when they possess an administrative apparatus which advances its claim to the monopoly of force in a given territory. Only with Kelsen (1922), who criticized the double perspective of Jellinek (which he called *Zweiseitentheorie*), was the state turned completely into a legal structure and as a consequence it disappeared as an entity different from the law which regulates the production and implementation of legal norms. Of all Kelsen's theses, the radical reduction of the state to its legal structure is the one that has fared worst. With the transformation of the pure state of law into the social state, the exclusively legal theory of the state was condemned as formalistic by jurists, whereas studies by political sociologists which see the state as a complex form of social organization (of which the law is but one constitutive element), have flourished.

Functionalism and Marxism

Among sociological theories of the state, two in particular have been predominant in recent years. Often the two have been in contention with one another, but more often they have ignored each other, proceeding along their respective paths as if oblivious of the other's existence. Marxist theory and functionalism, the latter dominant in American political science and with great influence in Europe, were accepted for years as political sciences *par excellence*. There are differences between the two theories, both with regard to their general conception of science and methodology. The essential difference, however, concerns the location of the state within the social system as a whole. The Marxian conception distinguishes in each society, at least at certain moments of economic development, between two elements which do not possess the same determining power or capacity to influence the development of the system and the transition from one system to another. These are the economic base and the superstructure. Political institutions, in a word the state, belong to the second moment. The underlying moment includes economic relations, which are characterized in any era by a given mode of production, and is the determining moment even if not always dominant, according to some interpretations. The functionalist conception, which derives from Parsons, views the complex global system as divided into four sub-systems (pattern maintenance, goal attainment, adaptation and integration), each of which is equally essential for the maintenance of social equilibrium and, to that extent, they are reciprocally interdependent. The function of goal attainment is attributed to the political sub-system. This is the same as saying that the political function exercised by the collection of institutions which constitute the state is one of the four fundamental functions of every social system.

It may be true that in the Marxian conception the relation between economic base and political superstructure is one of reciprocal action; nevertheless, the idea that the economic base is always what in the last instance determines remains an unshakeable one. To remove that idea is to remove one of the essential characteristics of Marxist theory. In functionalist theory there is no distinction of levels between the various functions which any social system cannot do without. If a pre-eminent function were to be attributed to any of the sub-systems it would be to the cultural, not to the economic, sub-system because the cohesiveness of any social group depends on adhesion to values and stabilized norms through which the processes of socialization (the internationalization of social values) on the one hand, and social control (observance of norms which regulate general behaviour) on the other, take place.

These two different, sometimes even opposed, conceptions can be reduced to the fundamental problems which they pose and which they mean to resolve. Whereas functionalist theory, especially in its Parsonian version, is obsessed with the Hobbesian theme of order, Marxist theory is obsessed with that of the collapse of order. This collapse is seen as the transition from one mode of production to another through the explosion of internal contradictions within the system, particularly contradictions between the forces of production and the relations of production. Whereas the first is concerned with the idea of social continuity, the second is essentially concerned with social change. On the one hand the changes that interest functionalist theory are those which occur within the system and which the system has the capacity to absorb through internal adjustments foreseen by the system itself. Marx and his followers, on the other hand, have always believed in the big change, which with a qualitative leap throws a system into crisis and creates a new one out of it. It is commonplace, but no less correct for all that, to say that the great division is between systems which favour the moment of cohesion and those which favour the moment of conflict: so-called integrationist versus so-called conflictualist systems. It would be difficult in the history of sociological thought to find two stronger archetypes of this dichotomy than Marxism and functionalism. It should be added that the functionalist system is, in some respects, analogous to the one against which Marx fought a major theoretical battle. This is the conception of the classical economists according to which civil society, notwithstanding its conflicts, obeys a kind of pre-established order, and enjoys the advantage of a mechanism, the market, which maintains equilibrium by continually adjusting competing interests.

In the past few years, the point of view that has prevailed in the characterization of the state is the systems-perspective that derives with some variations and without too much vigour from the theory of systems (above all, David Easton and Gabriel Almond). The relation between political institutions and the social system as a whole is represented as a questions-and-answer relation (input–output). The function of political institutions is to respond to demands originating from the social environment or, according to one current terminology, to convert questions into answers. The responses of political institutions are given in the form of collective decisions which are binding on the whole society. These responses in their turn affect changes in the societal environment. Due to the way answers are given, new demands are created in a process of continual change. This can be gradual, as when a correspondence exists between demands and responses, or abrupt when, due to an excess of demands over responses, the flow of feedback is interrupted. Thus existing political institutions, in failing to provide satisfactory responses, undergo a process of change which can result in their complete transformation.

The systems representation of the state is perfectly compatible with both the general theories of society discussed
above. Notwithstanding the different interpretations of the
function of the state in society, its systemic representation
is meant to propose a conceptual scheme for analysing how
political institutions function, and how they exercise their
specific function, whatever the various interpretations may
be.

State and society

What has changed, in fact completely reversed, in the
course of centuries of reflection on the problem of the state
is the relation between state and society. For centuries the
political organization was the object *par excellence* of all
reflection on the social life of humankind, on man as a
social animal, as *politikòn zôon* where *politikòn* includes
without differentiation the two contemporary meanings of
'social' and 'political'. This does not mean to say that
ancient thought did not highlight the existence of other
forms of human association, but the family was considered
by Aristotle as the embryonic and imperfect form of the
polis and he deals with it right at the beginning of the
Politics. As for other forms of society or *koinoníai* which
are constituted through agreement or necessity among
individuals with the intention of achieving particular aims,
these are dealt with by Aristotle in the chapter of the
Nicomachean Ethics devoted to friendship. In so far as
they are formed for the achievement of particular ends,
navigation by navigators, victory in war by armies, pleasure
or amusement by those who come together in banquets,
they are subordinated to political society, which does not
aim at a particular or momentary good, but at the general
good involving the entire life of man (1160a). The relation
between political society, which alone is the *societas perfecta*,
and particular societies is the relation between the whole
and its parts, with an all-encompassing *polis* encircling the
family and other associations. In all political writers, up to
and including Hegel, this relation between the state

and lesser, or partial, associations remained constant. In Hobbes's *Leviathan* (1651), besides the chapter on the family and patriarchical society, which is common to treatises of the period, there is also a chapter on partial associations (called in a Greek manner 'systems') with many examples and an accompanying typology which today would be one of the principal chapters in a sociological treatise.

The political theory of Hegel as propounded in Part Three of *The Philosophy of Right* (1821) is a theory of the state as the culminating moment of objective spirit, culminating in the sense that it resolves and surpasses the preceding moments of the family and civil society. It is here that we find, among other things, the treatment of corporations which are typical partial associations with particular ends, in the traditional sense. With the emancipation of bourgeois society (from the Marxian point of view), or industrial society (in the Saint-Simonian perspective), from the state, the relations between political institutions and society are inverted. Little by little society, in its various articulations, becomes the whole. The state, by contrast, narrowly seen as the coercive apparatus with which one sector of society exercises power over another, is reduced to a part. Up to now the course of humanity has been seen as a development from lesser societies such as the family to the state; now finally with the discovery on the one side of economic laws which allow people to live in harmony together with minimum need of a coercive apparatus and therefore of political power (Adam Smith), and on the other with the development of industrial organization together with scientists and industrialists who can do without Caesar's sword (Saint-Simon), we reach the stage when a reverse process will occur: the development away from an oppressive state towards a free society. From this inversion emerges one of the dominant ideas of the nineteenth century, one which is equally common to scientific and Utopian socialism, to the various forms of libertarian thought as well as liberal thought in its most radical expression: the inevitable extinction of the state, or at least its reduction to a minimum. As for approaches to the state, these became increasingly specialized compared to general approaches to society. A few years after the death of Hegel, Comte's *Cours de philosophie positive* appeared (1830–42), and in it culminated the general theory of society or sociology with the theme of the state constituting only a part. In Hegel's Germany, in the work of Lorenz von Stein, the general science of the state (*gesamte Staatswisssenschaft*) disappears and becomes merely *Staatswissenschaft* (as opposed to *Gesellschaftswissenschaft*, the science of society), increasingly restricted in its range and reduced to dealing with the state as distinct from global society. Today political sociology is a part of general sociology, and political science is one of the social sciences. The state as a political system is now a sub-system in relation to the social system.

Rulers and ruled

Along with the many ways of looking at the problem of the state – so far examined from the point of view of the object, of the method and of the conception of the social system – we should mention a generally neglected conflict which divides political doctrines into two opposing camps more than any other dichotomy: this refers to the opposition which originates in the different positions taken by writers on the fundamental political relation of rulers and ruled, or sovereign and subjects, or state and citizens, a relationship generally considered as a relation between superiors and inferiors. The exception is the radical democratic theory in which rulers and ruled are identified, at least ideally, as the same so that government becomes self-government. Looking at the political relation as a specific relation between two agents where one has the right to command and the other the duty to obey, the problem of the state can be seen from the point of view of either the ruler or of the ruled: *ex parte principis* or *ex parte populi*.

In fact, in the long tradition that goes from Plato's

Statesman to Machiavelli's *Prince*, from Xenophon's *Cyro-paedia* to Erasmus's *Princeps christianus*, political writers have envisaged the state chiefly from the point of view of the rulers. The essential themes of this tradition are: the art of good government; the virtues, capacities or abilities needed for good government: the various forms of government; the distinction between good and bad government; the phenomenology of tyranny in all its various forms; the rights, duties and prerogatives of rulers; the different functions of the state and the powers needed to discharge them adequately; the various branches of administration; fundamental concepts such as *dominium, imperium, maiestas, auctoritas, potestas* and *summa potestas*, all of which refer to just one half of the relationship (to the higher part which becomes the real subject of the relationship), the former becoming passive, matter rather than form. It was certainly not the case that the other perspective – political society seen from below, from the point of view of the interests, needs and rights, of the recipients of the benefits (or evils, according to the case) of government – was completely absent. However, the persistent use of certain metaphors – the shepherd which presupposes a flock, the captain (in the original sense of helmsman) which presupposes a crew, the parent which presupposes children needful of protection, the master which presupposes servants – shows more than any long analysis the prevalent meaning and direction of centuries of political discourse. Even the metaphor adopted by Plato (in the *Statesman*) of the ruler–weaver – 'the aim of the cloth of political action is a good weave' (311b) – does not escape from this perspective: the art of the weaver is to 'tell everyone which works are to be carried through to the end' (308e).

The beginning of the modern age saw a complete turnabout, with the discovery of the other side of the moon which up until then had remained hidden; to wit, new doctrines concerning the natural rights of the individual. These rights precede the formation of any political society and therefore of any structure of power that it might come to possess. Unlike the family or aristocratic society, political society begins to be understood predominantly (although there were precedents in the classical age) as the voluntary product of individuals, who decide in mutual agreement to live in society and set up a government. Johannes Althusius, one of the greatest architects of this new way of seeing things, defined politics in this manner: 'Politics is the art through which men join together with the aim of beginning, cultivating and maintaining between themselves, social life. For this reason it is defined as symbiotic' (1603, I). Althusius takes his point of departure from 'men' and proceeds through the work of men to the description of the political community. Aristotle's point of departure, and he was the standard authority for centuries, was exactly the opposite: 'It is evident', he wrote, 'that the State exists naturally [and as such is not established by men] but is anterior to each individual' (*Politics*, 1253a, 25).

What did this reversal of the starting-point involve, even if Althusius failed to follow through all of its consequences? It consisted in the importance attached to political problems other than those dealt with by writers who placed themselves *ex parte principis*: the liberty of citizens (in fact or in law, civil or political, negative or positive) rather than the powers of government, the well-being, prosperity and the happinesss of individuals taken one by one rather than the power of the state; the right of resistance to unjust laws rather than simply the duty of obedience (active or passive); political society seen as being composed of contrasting parts (parties not judged only as factions tearing the fabric of the state) rather than as a compact unity; the division, and the horizontal and vertical opposition, of the various centres of power as opposed to concentrated and centralized power; the merit of a government judged by the quantity of rights enjoyed by the individual rather than the degree of power of the rulers. For Locke the purpose of civil government is to guarantee property which he sees as an individual right preceding the birth of the state; for Spinoza and

Rousseau it is liberty, not the *libertas* which Hobbes read on the walls of fortified cities and interpreted correctly as independence from other cities (the self-sufficiency spoken of by Aristotle). The highest and most concrete expressions of this turnabout are the American and French Declarations of Rights, solemnly announcing the principle that government is for the individual and not the individual for the government: a principle which has influenced not just all later constitutions, but also thinking about the state and which has become, at least ideally, irreversible.

In political thought, at least since the French Revolution onwards, the greatest and most significant shift concerns the idea of change (in the sense used in Book V of Aristotle's *Politics*), from one form of government to another. Generally considered an evil (the logical conclusion of a political doctrine which for centuries esteemed and exalted stability and considered civil war the worst of evils), this passage came to acquire a positive value for the revolutionary movements which saw in change the beginning of a new era. But indeed, civil war represented the crisis of the state seen *ex parte principis*, whereas revolution, interpreted positively, represented the crisis of the state seen *ex parte populi*.

THE NAME AND THE THING

Origin of the name

It is undeniable that the word 'state' achieved its position through the diffusion and prestige of Machiavelli's *The Prince*. As is well known, the work begins as follows: 'All states and dominions which hold or have held sway over mankind are either republics or monarchies' (1513). This does not mean that the word was introduced by Machiavelli. Painstaking and wide-ranging research on the use of the word 'state' in fifteenth- and sixteenth-century language shows that the shift in the accepted meaning of the term *status*, from 'situation' to 'state' in the modern sense of the word, had already come about through the isolation of the first term of the classical expression *status rei publicae*. Machiavelli himself could not have used that phrase at the very beginning of his work if the word had not already had that current use.

Undoubtedly, it was through the author of *The Prince* that the term 'state' came gradually to substitute for the traditional term which had previously denoted the highest organization of a group of individuals on a territory possessed of the power of command: *civitas*, which corresponded to the Greek *polis*, and *res publica*, which Roman authors used to designate the totality of Roman political institutions. The length of this process is demonstrated by the fact that, even at the end of the sixteenth century, Jean Bodin could entitle his political treatise *De la république* (1576), although it deals with all forms of the state and not only republics. In the seventeenth century, Hobbes usually used the terms *civitas* (in his Latin works) and 'commonwealth' (in his English works) where the word state would appear today. Not that the Romans did not know and use the term *regnum* to refer to a system different from the *civitas* (ruled by the power of only one person). However, no matter how clear the distinction between government by one and government by a collective body, there was never a word used to describe the genus of which *res publica* and *regnum*, in the strict sense, were the species. *Res publica* continued to be used both for species and genus: *Cum penes unum est omnium summa rerum, regem illum unum vocamus et regnum eius rei publicae status* ('and so when the supreme authority is in the hands of one man we call him a king and the form of his state a kingship', Cicero, *De re publica*, I, 26, 42). The same Roman historian offered an extremely significant and apt example of the shift from one political regime to another; the transition from *regnum* to *res publica* and from *res publica* to *principatus*. During the reign of Caesar when Cicero wrote, 'we retain only the form of the commonwealth but the thing itself we have long since lost' (ibid., v, 1, 2), he showed himself perfectly aware of the ambiguous meaning of the term *res publica*. Clearly, in his mind, the distinction between 'republic' as a specific form of government (the form of government of 'republican' Rome) and other possible forms of government was very much to the fore. The one generic word known by the ancients for indicating the various forms of government was *civitas*.

However, in Machiavelli's time this must have seemed increasingly inadequate, especially to those speaking the vernacular. It failed to represent the reality of those political systems whose territory extended far beyond the walls of the city, including those republics which derived their name from a city. The republic of Venice is one example. The need for having a generic term more appropriate in the objective situation must have been stronger than the bonds of a long and authoritative tradition. From there the term 'state' underwent as yet unclear changes. It had the generic meaning of 'situation', and was beginning to refer to the condition of permanent and exclusive possession of a territory, and command of its inhabitants. This appears in the same piece by Machiavelli where the term 'state', barely introduced, is rapidly assimilated to the term dominion. While it is important to note the novelty of the use of the word 'state' as a generic term and 'republic' as a species term, and the consequent influence on current usage, it should be noted that even Machiavelli did not abandon the traditional meanings of these terms and their use continued to be widespread as can be seen in the passage from the *Discourses* where Machiavelli, taking Polybius for his guide, introduces the discourse on the forms of government: 'I agree with those who wrote of republics saying that they could be one of three states, called by them Principality, Aristocratic and Popular; and any group of people choosing an order for a city must turn to one of these, according to what seems to them the most appropriate' (1513–19).

Arguments in favour of discontinuity

The problem of the term 'state' would be less important if the introduction of the new term at the threshold of the modern age were not the occasion for claiming that it corresponded not only to the exigencies of lexical clarity, but also served the need to find a new name for a new reality: the reality of the modern state considered as a type of system quite different from those preceding it, and for which the old names were no longer suitable. It is a widely-held opinion of historians, lawyers and political writers that with Machiavelli there began not just the success of a word but also theorizing about a reality unknown to ancient writers, and of which the new word is a sign. Therefore it would be opportune only to speak of the state when referring to the political formation that originated in the crisis of medieval society, and not for preceding arrangements. In other words, the term 'state' should be used with caution for political organizations that existed before that system which was first called the 'state'. The new name is the name for a new entity. The debate has often assumed the form of replies to questions of this type: 'Did there exist a political society which could be called a "state" before the large territorial states with which the history of the modern State begins?'; or: 'Is the adjective "modern" necessary for distinguishing a reality that begins with the name "state" and for which, therefore, any other specification is useless?'; or: 'What is added to the meaning of "state" by the adjective "modern" that was not already implicit in the word's use by the ancients?'

Questions of this kind are linked to a much vaster problem, the range of answers to which is infinitely wide and radically contrasting: the problem of the origin of the state. There is a tendency among those historians who have described the formation of the large territorial states in terms of the dissolution and transformation of medieval society to identify a degree of discontinuity between the systems of the ancient world, or the Middle Ages, and those of the modern world. Consequently they see the state as a historical formation that has not always existed but has originated in a relatively recent epoch. There is no shortage of arguments in favour of this thesis. The strongest posits an inexorable process concentrating the power of command over a vast territory which is brought about by the monopolization of certain essential functions relating to the maintenance of internal and external order; for example, the production of law by whoever holds sovereign power (which is not custom but an emanation of the sovereign's will), and the coercive apparatus necessary for the enforcement of the law against unwilling persons, as well as through the reorganization of the imposition and collection of taxes necessary for the effective exercise of these augmented powers. Max Weber, who described this phenomenon with extraordinary lucidity, saw in the formation of the modern state the phenomenon of the expropriation of the means of service, such as weapons, on the part of public power which proceeds at the same rate as the expropriation from artisans of the means of production by those who possess capital. It is from this observation that the now commonplace Weberian conception derives, the definition of the modern state in terms of two necessary constitutive elements: the presence of an administrative apparatus which has the function of taking care of the provision of public services, and the legitimate monopoly of force.

Whatever the arguments might be for or against the continuity of a society's political organization, the question of whether the state has always existed, or whether it only emerged during a certain era, depends entirely on the definition of the state. The choice of definition depends on pragmatic criteria rather than truth. It is known that the greater the number of connotations attached to a concept, the narrower is the range which it denotes (its extension). Whoever claims as the constitutive elements of the state a certain administrative apparatus and the implementation of certain functions which only the modern state undertakes,

must necessarily claim that the Greek *polis* is not a state,
that feudal society did not have a state, and so on. The
real problem which those interested in understanding the
phenomenon of political systems must confront is not that
the state has only existed since the modern age, but that
if there are analogies and differences between the so-called
modern state and previous systems then which of these
should be highlighted whatever name you wish to give to
the different systems. Those who claim that it is only
possible to speak of the state when speaking of the political
system dealt with by Bodin, Hobbes and Hegel do so
because they see more discontinuity than continuity, more
differences than analogies. Those who make no distinction
between Bodin's 'state' and the Greek *polis* see more
analogies than differences, more continuity than discontinuity. Putting the question in these terms means going
beyond dictionary definitions and describing the changes
that have occurred in the shift from one system to another.
This means looking at what has remained and what has
changed, the elements of continuity and of discontinuity,
without being blinded by the appearance of a new name.

Arguments in favour of continuity

The arguments in favour of continuity are as strong as those
in favour of discontinuity. Above all there is the claim that
a political treatise such as Aristotle's, dedicated to the
analysis of the Greek city, has lost none of its descriptive
and explanatory power when confronted with the political
systems that follow it. One thinks of the typology of
governmental forms which has come down to us, and which
was adopted, albeit with corrections and adaptations, by
those political writers who were interested in the modern
state. Equally one thinks of Aristotle's definition of
'constitution' (*politeia*) as an arrangement of the magistrature, which constitutes the organization of the city, the
distribution of the tasks and the distinction of functions,
which permits an illuminating comparative analysis with

modern political systems. Furthermore one thinks of the analysis of change, the various modes of transition from one form of government to another to which Book V is dedicated, which is as useful as ever for contemporary political analysis. This is borne out by the fact that the relations between the Greek cities, characterized by war, reprisals, truces and peace treaties, could reproduce themselves on a quantitively higher but not qualitatively different level in the relations between states in the modern age. If you read Grotius's *De iure belli ac pacis libri tres* (1625) you should not be surprised when you confront a myriad of examples of *ius genituum* taken from the ancient world when modern states – in the sense modernists have given this expression – did not yet exist. Thucydides' *Histories* does for external relations what Aristotle's *Politics* does for internal relations. They remain inexhaustible sources of instruction and of points of reference and comparison. Machiavelli himself read and commented on Roman history not as a historian but as a student of politics looking for examples to apply to the states of his time. The study of Roman history through the great historians, from Livy to Tacitus, has always been one of the principal sources for those political treatises which accompanied the formation and growth of the modern state. Even Montesquieu wrote his *Considérations sur les causes de la grandeur des Romains et de leur décadence* (1734). Rousseau dedicated the last part of *The Social Contract* (1762) to an examination of Roman dictatorship and the censor not in order to show off facile and useless learning but to demonstrate its perennial vitality. This continued reflection on ancient history and institutions would be difficult to explain had there been, at a certain moment in historical development, a shift leading to a wholly new type of political and social organization so incomparable with the past as alone to merit the name of 'state'.

The same argument can be made, and has been made, for that long period of history from the fall of the Roman Empire to the birth of the large territorial states. The question of continuity is particularly interesting in this context, whether at the beginning with regard to the society and the economic and social institutions of the latter days of the Empire which raises the question: 'Does the low empire already contain symptoms of the Middle Ages, or did the High Middle Ages preserve remains of classic antiquity?'; or at the end in the process of the ever-increasing concentration of power from which originates the idea of the state that has lasted until today. Nothing demonstrates the relativity of the notion of continuity more than the dispute about that long age of transition and supposed decadence (Vico's 'barbarism returned') which constitutes the Middle Ages. But continuity of what: continuity of political institutions such as the organization of central power or of economic institutions such as the great landed properties and the mode of cultivating the earth? Is there any continuity between Roman cities and medieval ones, between the *collegia* and the corporations? Above all, then, with regard to political organization, is it really possible to talk of the 'state', implying as it does the idea of unity of power on a given territory, in the fractionalized and multi-centred societies of the first medieval centuries, the time of barbarian rulers when the principal functions now usually attributed to the state (and used to connote it) were performed by peripheral powers?

In such societies there was no distinction either at the highest or the lowest levels between genuinely political power and economic power. Equally, relations of public law were regulated by typically private legal institutions including the contract which is a relationship of *do ut des*. Personal relations prevailed over territorial ones, according to the noted distinction between *Personen Verbandstaat* and the *Institutioneller Flaechenstaat*. Here, too, the abstract idea of the state, so well named in the Latin *res publica*, disappeared and was identified more and more with the personal power of an individual, invested by divine will of God with command over others. Nevertheless, even at the height of the Middle Ages the idea of *regnum* and *imperium* did not disappear: that is, of a power which alone is authorized to exercise force in the last instance, because its supreme purpose is the maintenance of peace and the exercise of justice (*rex a recte regendo*), two functions which could not possibly be fulfilled without the possession of superior and legitimate coercive power; and really because as such, as Marc Bloch observed, it preserved for centuries a vigour which went beyond the feudal social system and became one of the principles on which approaches to the state are based to this day.

Nevertheless, it was during the Middle Ages that jurists elaborated a legalistic conception of the state which was not unlike Roman political theory (one remembers the *coetus multitudinis iuris consensu* of Cicero). The first commentators on the *Corpus iuris* elaborated the relation between *lex* and *rex*, the theory of sovereignty as independence (*superiorem non recognoscens*) and therefore as the power to dictate laws without authorization (the city *sibi princeps* which reproduces the meaning of the Greek *autokrates*) and which, through the different interpretations of the *lex regia de imperio*, brought into discussion the problem of the foundation of power. The distinction between monarch and tyrant belongs to the medieval approach, and through it the problem of good government becomes one of the enduring themes of political theory. It is one of the principal themes of John of Salisbury's *Polycraticus* (twelfth century), followed by one of the best known tracts of Bartolo di Sassoferrato (*Tractatus de regimine civitatis*, fourteenth century) and Coluccio Salutati (*De tyranno*, late fourteenth century) with which one arrives at the dawn of the modern age. Finally, it is through the debate on the foundation of power (posed in legal terms) that the ideas of the social contract and the contract of submission were born, which were to inspire the contractualistic doctrines which played a great part in the debate on the origin and foundation of the state in the modern age. These doctrines were rejected during the nineteenth century but today they have become of great relevance because they serve to explain the mediating function of the contemporary state in great social conflicts, more so than the organic theories of the state in whose name contractualism was abandoned.

When was the state born?

Those who hold that the concept of the state and the associated theory must be sufficiently broad to include political arrangements different and antecedent to the modern state have no difficulty in dissociating the origin of the name from the origin of the thing. However, they cannot avoid the problem of whether the state has always existed or whether it is a historical phenomenon that appears at a certain moment in human evolution. A recurring thesis runs with extraordinary continuity through the whole history of political thought: the state, understood as the political system of a community, is born with the dissolution of the primitive community based on kinship ties and from the formation of larger communities, derived from the union of family groups for reasons of internal survival (nourishment) and external survival (defence). While for some contemporary historians, as has been noted above, the birth of the state signals the beginning of the modern age, according to this older and more common interpretation the birth of the state marks the passage from the primitive age, divided into savagery and barbarism, to the civil age where civil stands for both 'civic' and 'civilized' (Adam Ferguson). In the entire natural law tradition, the state of nature which precedes civil society is always represented as a purely hypothetical state of isolation or as a state in which primitive people would have lived and savage people still live in the wild. In both cases it is not accidental that the condition in which people lived before the appearance of the state is called, in antithesis to the state of nature, *societas civilis* (where civil means both not-natural and not-savage). For Vico the first form of the state in the proper sense of the word is preceded by the savage condition (asocial) and by the state of families, which is a social but not a political condition, and is a consequence of the revolt of the servants when the heads of families were forced to unite and breathe life into the first form of the state, the aristocratic republic.

A noted variation is provided in the thesis of the first anthropologists, such as Charles Morgan, and taken up and popularized by Engels, who transplanted it to the Marxist theory of the state as an instrument of class domination. For Engels, too, the state originates in the dissolution of aristocratic society founded on family bonds, and the birth of the state marks the passage from barbarism to civility. In this context, the word 'civil' is used as Rousseau used it, with a negative connotation. Engels's differs from all preceding interpretations of the state, including Morgan's, by offering an exclusively economic interpretation. It brings to mind Rousseau's imaginative reconstruction which lays the foundation of civil society in the act of the first person to enclose an estate saying: 'This is mine': that is, from the institution of private property. For Engels, in the primitive community, whether it is the *gens* of the Romans or the Iroquoi tribe, the regime of collective property is in force. With the birth of private property the division of labour is born. With the division of labour, society divides itself into classes: the class of proprietors and the class of owners of nothing. From this division into classes political power is born. The state's essential function is to maintain the dominance of one class over the other, even to the extent of using force, preventing a class-divided society from turning into a state of permanent anarchy.

Agreeing with and following this tradition of thought, the problem of the origin of the state in primitive societies is one of the great debates in cultural anthropology: were primitive societies acquainted with systems of living together that might be called states, or should they be considered more as 'societies without states' or, in the polemic words of Clastres, as a 'society against the state'? This debate, too, is to a large extent nominalist in that it depends on the multiplicity of meanings of the term 'state'. A solution which is adopted more and more by anthropologists is to avoid speaking of the state. The term is too compromised by the use made of it to designate the modern state. Instead, we can speak of political organization or political system (as in the fundamental work in this field by Evans-Pritchard and Fortes, 1940). This is only an apparent solution as it does not get round the task of delimiting and defining the concept of the political. This is no less ambiguous than the concept of the state, even if it offers the advantage of traditionally and conventionally possessing a wider connotation; the Greek *polis* need not enter into the definition of the state but it would not be possible to leave it out of the definition of the political system.

The choice between the statements, 'there are primitive societies without a state in so far as they do not have a political organization', and 'there are primitive societies which, although they are not states, have a political organization' depends on an initial agreement on the meaning of terms like 'political' and 'state'. Once again, what matters is the analysis of the similarities and differences between different forms of social organization, how one changes into another, and when one is confronted with a formation which presents sufficiently different characteristics from the preceding one as to warrant the attribution of a different name or a different specification of the same name. For example, when a scholar distinguishes between three types of stateless societies which are called, respectively, 'society with minimal government', 'with diffuse government' and 'with expanding government', it is not excluded that these societies can be considered political societies as the use of the term 'government' makes understood (La Mair). At this point the following problem is posed: are there primitive societies which are not political organizations in even the widest sense of the term? To give another example, those who distinguish leaderless societies from those with a leader see the former as non-political because their criterion is a certain concentration of power and the need for guidance at the top. If, by contrast, they identify the state mainly with centralized power but then introduce an ulterior distinction between coercive power, using force to make itself felt, and the power of words, of gestures and/or of symbols, it is possible to claim that only the first are political societies.

THE STATE AND POWER

Theories of power

Before the appearance and the current use of the term 'state', the problem of the distinction between political systems and state was not even posed. But the identification of the political sphere with the sphere of the state continued well beyond the introduction of the term 'state'. From the *Politica methodice digesta* of Johannes Althusius (1603) to Heinrich von Treitschke's *Politik* (1894–6) until Croce's *Politica in nuce* (1925), the approach to the subject of the state continued to be described as politics, originally derived from that particular form of political system which is the *polis*. In the last few years, moreover, students of political phenomena have abandoned the term state and substituted for it the more comprehensive term 'political system'. One of the advantages of this expression is that it has a more neutral value than the word state which, on the one hand, reflects a deification and, on the other, a demonization by conservatives and revolutionaries respectively of the concentrated systems of power which have been called by that name ever since Machiavelli coined it.

'State' and 'political' have it in common (and it is the reason for their interchangeability) that they refer to phenomena of power. From the Greek *krátos* (strength, power) and *arké* (authority) come the names of the ancient forms of government: 'aristocracy', 'democracy', 'ochlocracy', 'monarchy', 'oligarchy' and all the words which were gradually moulded to indicate forms of power:

'physiocracy', 'bureaucracy', 'party rule', 'polyarchy', 'exarchy', and so on. There is no political theory which does not start either directly or indirectly from a definition of power and from an analysis of the phenomenon of power. By long tradition the state is defined as the bearer of *summa potestas*; and the analysis of the state almost completely turns into the study of the various 'powers' that belong to the sovereign. The theory of the state revolves around the theory of the three powers (legislative, executive and judiciary) and of their relations. In a classical text of our times, *Power and Society* by Lasswell and Kaplan (1952), the political process is defined as the 'formation, distribution and exercise of power'. If the theory of the state can be considered as a part of political theory, political theory can, in turn, be considered as part of the theory of power.

In political philosophy the problem of power is presented from three points of view on the basis of which three fundamental theories of power can be distinguished: substantialist, subjective and relational. In the substantialist theory, power is thought of as something which can be possessed and used like any other good. Hobbes's theory is typical of this approach according to which 'the power of a man . . . is his present means to obtain some future apparent good' (1651). Whether these means are natural endowments, such as strength and intelligence, or whether they are acquired, like wealth, does not change the chief sense of power understood as something which is used to achieve the object of desire. Bertrand Russell's well-known definition, according to which power consists in 'the production of desired effects', is analogous (1938) and by the terms of this definition can assume three forms. Physical and constrictive power, which has its most concrete visible expression in military terms; psychological power based on threats of punishment or promises of reward, which mainly exist in the economic field; and mental power, which is exercised through persuasion or dissuasion and which is, in its elementary form, present in education in all societies.

A typical subjectivistic interpretation of power is Locke's (1694, II, xxi), whose understanding of power is not as something used to achieve aims but the capacity of the subject to obtain certain effects. To say that 'fire has the power to melt metals' is the same as to say that sovereigns have the power to make laws and in so doing to influence the conduct of their subjects. This way of interpreting power is that adopted by lawyers to define subjective right: to say that subjects have a subjective right is to say that the legal system has given them the power to obtain certain effects. However, the most widespread interpretation in contemporary political discourse is the third, which goes back to the relational concept of power, whereby power means a relation between two subjects/agents in which the first obtains from the second behaviour that otherwise would not have occurred. The most noted and the most synthetic of relational definitions is Robert Dahl's (1963): 'Influence [a broader concept which the concept of power enters into] is a relation between actors in which one actor induces other actors to behave in a manner in which otherwise they would not behave.' Defined in this manner as the relation between two agents, power is closely linked to freedom so that the definition of one is the negation of the other: 'The power of A implies the non-freedom of B'; 'the freedom of A implies the non-power of B.'

The forms of power and political power

Once the concept of the state has been reduced to that of the political and the concept of politics to that of power, the problem becomes one of distinguishing political power from all other power relations. Political theory has been perennially concerned with this theme with infinite variations. The classical typology handed down for centuries has been Aristotle's, whereby three types of power are distinguished on the basis of the sphere in which it is exercised: the power of parents over their children, of the master over his slaves and of the rulers over the ruled.

Aristotle adds that it is possible to distinguish between the
three forms of power on the basis of who gains from
exercising it. Parental power is exercised in the interest of
the children; the master's, or despotic power, is in the
interest of the master; political power is in the interests of
those who govern and those who are governed (so that the
corrupt form of political regime is where the ruler, having
become a tyrant, rules only in his or her own interest).
This typology has political relevance because it has been
used to propose two schemes of reference for defining
corrupt forms of government. The first is paternalistic or
patriarchal government, whereby the sovereign behaves like
a father towards his subjects and where the subjects are
always treated like minors. The most celebrated criticism
of this form of government was made by Locke in the
second of his two *Treatises on Government* (1690) in his
polemic against Robert Filmer's *Patriarcha* (1680). This was
taken up by Kant in his criticism of the eudemonological
state which is concerned with the happiness of its subjects
instead of limiting itself to guaranteeing their liberty. The
second form is despotic government, where the sovereign
treats his or her subjects like slaves whose rights are not
recognized. This form of government was already clearly
pointed out by Aristotle, who considered it suitable for
peoples that were naturally slavish like Orientals and bar-
barians, who tolerate oppressive power without complaint
or rebellion and which received full recognition (again
referring to Oriental peoples) in Hegel and Montesquieu.

The tripartite division of forms of power into parental,
despotic and civil is one of the *topoi* of both classical and
modern political power. Hobbes, in his political works,
deals with family and patriarchal government before dealing
with civil power. Locke begins the Second Treatise by a
proposal to distinguish between the power of a father over
his sons and that of a galley captain over the galley slaves
(which is the modern form of slavery) from civil government.
But Locke's approach can be distinguished from Aristotle's
by the different criterion of distinction which have to do

with the different foundation of the three types of powers. Today one would say the different principles of legitimacy: paternal power has a natural foundation in that it originates in reproduction; despotic power is a consequence of the right to punish those held guilty of a grave crime and therefore open to an equally grave punishment such as slavery. Civil power, alone among the other forms of power, is founded on the express or tacit consent of those at whom it is directed. As everyone can see, it is a question of the three classical forms of the foundation of every obligation: *ex natura, ex delicto* and *ex contractu.*

This classical division, notwithstanding its success, does not allow one to distinguish political from other forms of power. The two criteria – the Aristotelian, based on interest, and the Lockian, based on the principle of legitimacy – are evaluative and not analytic in so far as they serve to distinguish political power as it should be and not as it is; the good forms from the corrupt forms. Both Aristotle and Locke must recognize that there are governments in which power is exercised in one of the other two forms. A realistic theory of political power as a form of power distinct from every other form of power can be constructed, according to the medieval jurists, in the elaboration of the concept of sovereignty or *summa potestas*. While ancient society only recognized one perfect association – the state which embraced all other lesser associations – medieval society recognised two: the state and the church. The age-old dispute about the pre-eminence of one or the other required a delimitation of the competence and therefore of dominion of the two spheres, and consequently of the specific characteristics of the two *potestates*. The distinction between the *vis directiva*, which is the prerogative of the church, and the *vis coactiva*, which is the prerogative of the state, became *communis opinio*. In contrast to the spiritual *potestà* and its claims, the defenders and holders of *potestà temporale* tended to attribute to the state the right and exclusive power of exercising physical force over the inhabitants of a given territory, leaving to the church the right and the power to teach the true religion and moral precepts and to direct consciences towards spiritual things, above all the salvation of the soul. Political power became so identified with the exercise of force that it was defined as that power which, in order to obtain the desired results (taking the Hobbesian definition), has the right to make use, if only in the last instance, of force. Here the criterion for distinguishing between political power and religious power is again the means adopted for imposing it: spiritual power principally uses psychological means even when it employs the threat of punishment or the promise of other-worldly rewards; political power makes use of physical means such as the use of arms.

Physical force is a necessary but not a sufficient condition in the definition of political power. According to the doctrine confirmed in the great controversy between state and church, the state is distinguished from the church by the exercise of force. However, another no less decisive controversy for defining political power is the apparent opposition of the *regna* to universal empire, *civitates* to the *regna*. Here we have another problem. It is not a question of the right to use force but the *exclusivity* of this right on a given territory. The sovereign is the one with the exclusive right to use force on a given territory. Whoever has the exclusive power to use force on given territory is the sovereign. Given that force is the most resolute way for one person to exercise dominion over another, whoever retains the use of these means to the exclusion of everyone else within certain borders possesses sovereignty in the sense of *summa potestas*, of supreme power: *summa* in the sense of *superiorem non recognoscens*, supreme in the sense that if force is a necessary condition of political power then its exclusive use is a sufficient condition. There are anticipatory forms of the concept of sovereignty (which became, in the use of modern writers, the fundamental concept for the definition of the state) in the distinction between the *civitates superiorem recognoscentes* and *superiorem non recognoscentes* of medieval lawyers who defended the legal and therefore political autonomy of the cities, and the principle *rex in regno suo imperator*, asserted by the French lawyers, who defended the sovereignty of the king in France against the claims of the emperor.

Jean Bodin, considered *the* theorist of sovereignty (in reality he is more than just the theorist: he is the authoritative expounder of a concept that has a long and solid tradition behind it), defines the state as 'the lawful rule by sovereign power of many families and of what is common to them' and sovereign power as 'absolute and enduring power' (1576) where 'absolute' means that it is subject to no laws but the natural and divine and 'enduring' that it succeeds in consistently getting its orders obeyed, thanks also to its monopoly of coercive power. The theme of the exclusivity of force as the characteristic of political power is the Hobbesian theme *par excellence*. The change from the state of nature to the state means the change from a condition in which everyone uses force indiscriminately against everyone else to the condition in which the right to use force belongs only to the sovereign. Beginning with Hobbes, political power takes on a connotation that remains constant until today. When Hegel, in his youthful *The Constitution of Germany* (1799–1802), complains that Germany is no longer a state, he begins by saying that 'a group of men can only call themselves a state if they unite for the common defence of everything that is their property', and later repeats: 'for a group of men to form a state it is necessary that they set up a common military apparatus and a state power.' Weber, using the language of economics, defines the state as the possessor of the monopoly of legitimate physical coercion. For Kelsen, the state is a coercive order, in particular: 'The state is a political organisation because it is a system which regulates the use of force and because it monopolises the use of force' (1945). In a widely used manual of political science one reads: 'We agree with Max Weber that legitimate physical force is the thread that runs through the action of the political system' (Almond and Powell 1966).

The three forms of power

From the point of view of the various criteria that have been adopted to distinguish between the various forms of power, the definition of political power as that type of power which can, in the last instance, have recourse to force (and is capable of doing so because it has a monopoly of it), is a definition that looks to the means used by those holding power to obtain the desired effects. The criterion of the means is the most widely used because it allows the construction of a typology that is at the same time both simple and illuminating: the so-called typology of the three powers, economic, ideological and political or, in other words, of wealth, knowledge and force. Economic power makes use of the possession of certain goods that are necessary or seen as such, in a condition of scarcity, in order to induce non-possessors to behave in a certain manner (generally the performance of useful work). There resides, in the possession of the means of production, an enormous source of power on the part of those who possess them over non-possessors, precisely in the specific sense of the capacity to determine the behaviour of others. In any society where there are proprietors and non-proprietors, the power of the proprietors derives from their ability to make non-proprietors (or those possessing only their own labour power) work for the proprietors in the conditions they stipulate. Ideological power is that which avails itself of the possession of certain forms of knowledge or doctrine, or even of information or codes of conduct in order to exercise an influence on the behaviour of others and to induce the members of a group to perform or not perform an action. The social importance of those who know derives from this type of conditioning – whether they be the priests of traditional societies or the scientists, technicians or so-called 'intellectuals' of secular societies – because it is through the knowledge that they diffuse or the values that they preach and inculcate that the socialization needed by every social group to stick together takes place. What these three forms of power have in common is that they jointly contribute to the institution and maintenance of a society of unequals: divided into weak and strong on the basis of the first, rich and poor on the basis of the second, and erudite and ignorant on the basis of the third; generically, between superiors and inferiors.

Above all, the definition of political power as the power whose specific means is force helps to explain why it is always looked upon as the ultimate power, the power whose possession indicates the dominant group in any society. Coercive power, in fact, is the power every social group needs to defend itself from external attacks or to prevent its own internal disintegration. In the relations between members of the same social group, not forgetting the state of subordination that expropriation of the means of production brings about in the expropriated, and notwithstanding the passive adhesion to handed-down values by the addressees of communications coming from the ruling class, only the use of physical force serves to prevent insubordination and to suppress every form of disobedience. In the relations between social groups, quite apart from the pressure exercised by the threat or execution of economic sanctions in order to induce the enemy group to desist from a course of action claimed to be harmful or offensive (in the relations between groups the effects of ideological conditioning count for less), the decisive instrument for the imposition of will is force: that is, war.

This distinction between three principal types of social power, although expressed in different ways, is an almost constant fact in contemporary social theories in which the social system as a whole is, directly or indirectly, articulated into three sub-systems: the organization of productive forces, the organization of consensus and the organization of coercive power. Even Marxist theory can be interpreted in this sense: the real base consists of the economic system while the superstructure, divided into two distinct moments, consists of the ideological system and the legal–political system (to which Marx, it should not be forgotten, attributes the repressive aspect, highlighting especially the coercive apparatus). The Gramscian system is more obviously tripartite as the superstructural moment divides into two moments: the moment of hegemony or of consensus which is called civil society, and the moment of domination or of force (called the state). Moreover, for centuries political writers have distinguished spiritual power (which today would be called ideological) from temporal power, and they have always interpreted temporal power as being constituted by the conjunction of *dominium*, the power over things constituted by economic power, with the *imperium*, which is the power of command over others and which is constituted by political power in the strict sense.

Both in the traditional dichotomy and in the Marxian one, three forms of power are found because the second term is correctly interpreted as being made up of two moments. The essential difference lies in the fact that in traditional theory the principal power is represented by ideological power in the sense that politico-economic power is conceived as being dependent on the spiritual, while in Marxian theory the principal power is economic in so far as ideologies and political institutions have the function of guaranteeing the continued existence of definite relations of production (at least until the point where the contradictions explode at a certain moment of development and produce change). At the beginning of the modern age is Hobbes's exemplary *De Cive* (1642) which is divided into three parts: *libertas, potestas* and *religio* which correspond respectively to the sphere of natural liberty where exchange relations take place and in which political power should intervene as little as possible (some, like MacPherson, see in Hobbes's state of nature a prefiguration of market society). The second corresponds to political power which possesses the two swords of justice and of war, and the third to spiritual power whose task is essentially teaching. For Hobbes, political power is power *par excellence* which, legitimated by a specific delegation of isolated and terrorized individuals, driven by necessity out of the state of nature, controls both spiritual and economic power. In this aspect as well, Hobbes can be considered the first and greatest theorist of the state: that is to say of the state whose formation is accompanied by the persistent idea of the primacy of the political.

The primacy of the political

The different relations between the three powers and the different ways of arranging them hierarchically are amongst the most persistent traits of the main currents of political theory and philosophy of history. The primacy of politics, which marks out modern political theory from Machiavelli to Hegel, is opposed both to the primacy of spiritual power which distinguishes the medieval age of the great controversies between state and church and which the Roman church and other churches have never given up, and the primacy of economic power whose discovery coincides with the birth of the bourgeois world and the beginning of theorizing on the capitalist mode of production.

Strictly connected to the ideal of the primacy of the political is the doctrine of *raison d'état* which, not coincidentally, was born and developed alongside the theory of the modern state. One of the forms in which the primacy of the political manifests itself is the independence of political from moral judgement, or even the superiority of the first over the second: that there exists a *raison d'état* separate from the reasoning of individuals means that the state, or more concretely the politician, is free to pursue aims without having to take into account the moral precepts which bind any individual in his or her relations with others. The subordination of political action to moral laws which are the precepts of the dominant religion reflects the primacy of the spiritual: a subordination which is reflected in the figure of the Christian prince. To the conception of the primacy of the political corresponds, instead, the doctrine of necessary immorality or amorality of political action

which must aim at its own purposes, the *salus rei publicae*,
without feeling itself bound and encumbered by obstacles
of another nature: a primacy reflected in the figure of the
Machiavellian prince whose means used to win and conquer
the state are always, no matter what they are, 'judged
honourable and praised by all' (*The Prince*, 1513, ch. 18).
In Hegel's *Philosophy of Right* (which completes, just as
Hobbes initiated, the theory of the modern state), the ultimate moment of the Objective Spirit, which covers the
traditional territory of practical philosophy, is not morality
but ethics, of which the supreme figure is the state.
Confronting the classical theme of the distinction between
morality and politics (that is, *raison d'état*), Hegel expresses
with maximum force the idea of the primacy of the second
over the first in a passage which with good reason could
be considered the quintessence of this idea and which
contains the principal argument for its justification: 'The
good of the State has a completely different right from the
good of an individual', because the state which is the
'ethical substance' 'has its existence (that is, its law),
immediately, in a concrete and not an abstract existence
. . . and only this concrete existence, and not one of the
general propositions taken for moral precepts, can be the
principle of its action and behaviour' (*The Philosophy of
Right*, 1821, 337a). What does this passage mean? It means
that the principle of action of the state must be sought in
the same necessity of being, of an existence which is the
same condition of existence (and not just of the existence
but also of the liberty and well-being) of individuals. This
may be proven by the fact that the tribunal which judges
the action of the state is not the external one instituted by
the state itself in order to judge the actions of its subjects
or that which each individual erects in his or her own mind
– conscience or God – but the tribunal of universal History,
the subjects of which are not individuals but states.

THE FOUNDATION OF POWER

The problem of legitimacy

Alongside the problem of the definition of political power and of the characteristics which distinguish it from other forms of power there is also the question of its justification. The problem of the justification of power stems from the question: 'Given that political power is the power that deploys the exclusive use of force within a definite social group, is force enough to make it accepted by those on whom it is exercised, to induce its addressees to obey it?' A question like this can have, and has had, two answers depending on whether it is interpreted as a question about what power actually is or what it ought to be. As often happens in the study of political problems even these two answers are confused, so that it is not possible to say whether the question is one of the relationship between power and force, or of the problem of the mere effectiveness (in the sense that a power founded on force alone cannot last) or also a problem of legitimacy (in the sense that a power founded on force alone may be considered effective but not legitimate). It is one thing to assert that political power cannot be just strength alone in the sense that it is not *possible*, another that it cannot be strength alone in the sense that it is not *right*. From the point of view of the addressees of power the same problem is posed as the problem of political obligation. But the problem of political obligation can be posed as the problem of the reasons why the commands of holders of a certain type of power should be obeyed or as the determination of the cases in which they have to be obeyed from those in which disobedience or passive obedience is correct.

As has already been said above, classical political theory, taking as its task the posing of the problem of the foundation of power, tended to deny that a power which is only strong, independently of the fact that it might be capable of lasting, could be justified. Whence comes the distinction, which is no longer analytical but evaluative, between legitimate and illegitimate power based on the customary argument, 'if power is founded exclusively on force then how can we distinguish political power from that of a band of robbers?'

This problem was stated concisely by St Augustine in a celebrated passage which has provoked innumerable commentaries: 'Without justice what in reality would kingdoms be but bands of robbers?' This passage is followed by the no less celebrated exchange of jokes between Alexander and the pirate: 'Having asked him why he infested the sea the pirate replied to the king: "for the same reason that you infest the earth; but because I do so with a little fleet I am called a pirate, while you, because you do it with a large fleet, you are called an emperor"' (*De civitate Dei*, IV, 4, 1–15). Two of the most famous books of political theory, Plato's *Republic* and Rousseau's *Social Contract*, begin with a debate on the relation between justice and force in which Socrates and Rousseau each reject the thesis that 'might is right'. Rousseau, too, uses the example of the brigand: 'If a brigand surprises me in the middle of a forest I would not only be forced to give him my purse but would I also be obliged in conscience to give it to him if I could hide it? Because, in the end, even the pistol he has in his hand is a form of power' (1762). When Bodin has to define the state he defines it as 'the *lawful* [in French *droit*, in Latin *legitimus*] rule which is exercised' (1576). Hobbes affirmed that for the security of its subjects, which is the supreme end of the state and therefore of the institution of political power, it is necessary that someone, whether an actual person or an assembly 'legitimately retains the ultimate power in the State' (1642). Moreover, it is on this basis of the attribution of an ethical or legal character to power that the distinction between good political power and bad political power, between sovereign and tyrant (where tyrant signifies the usurpation of power and not bad government as in classical antiquity) has existed for centuries: a distinction which has important consequences for the problem of political obligation so that Hobbes, the theorist of absolute obedience, affirms that the usurper (that is, the illegitimate prince) must be treated as an enemy.

The fact that supreme power (that is, political power) must have an ethical justification (or, which is the same thing, a legal foundation) has given rise to various principles of legitimacy: that is, of the various ways in which it is sought to provide a justification for the power-holder's right to command and for the subject's duty to obey; that which Gaetano Mosca called in the useful expression 'the political formula', explaining that:

it has happened in the limited number of societies arrived at a certain level of culture, that the political class does not exclusively justify its power solely on the grounds of possessing it but seeks to give it a moral and legal basis, making it originate as a necessary consequence of doctrines and beliefs generally recognised and accepted in the society that it directs. (1896)

Mosca only recognized two political formulas: one which derives power from the authority of God and another which derives it from the power of the people. Although considering them mere fictions he thought that they corresponded to a real need, the need to govern and to feel oneself governed 'not on the basis of material and intellectual force alone, but also on the grounds of a moral principle' (Mosca 1896).

The various principles of legitimacy

In reality there have been historically more principles of legitimacy adopted than the two mentioned by Mosca. Without any claim to be comprehensive we can distinguish between at least six which can be grouped together as antithetical pairs of the three great unifying principles, will, nature and history. The two principles of legitimacy which are connected to a superior will are those mentioned by Mosca: the governors receive their power from the will of God or of the people. The classic formula for this type of legitimation is Hobbes's: 'Authority and not Reason makes the Law.' But what is the ultimate source of authority? In a pyramidal conception of authority the ultimate authority is the will of God. In an ascending conception where power proceeds from the base to the apex, authority is ultimately the will of the people. However, the two principles, although antithetical, become in some versions mutually reinforcing: *vox populi vox Dei*. Naturalistic doctrines which originate in the various forms of natural law have always been opposed to voluntaristic doctrines. These have also been presented in apparently antithetical forms: nature as *krátos*, the original force according to the prevalent classical conception of power, and nature as rational order where the law of nature is identified with the law of reason according to the prevalent interpretation of modern natural law. To appeal to nature as the basis of power in the first version means that the right to command of one and the duty to obey of the others derives from the ineluctable fact that there are naturally, and therefore independently of human will, weak and strong, knowing and ignorant; or, in other words, individuals and even peoples suited to command and individuals and peoples capable only of obeying. Appealing to nature as a rational order means instead justifying power on the ability of the sovereign to identify and apply natural laws which are the laws of reason. For Locke the main duty of government is to make possible, through the exercise of coercive power, the observation of the laws of nature; which would have been respected without government had it not been that all people are not reasonable. Because people are not rational, Locke needs consensus to found the state, but that same consensus – or rather the agreement necessary to leave the state of nature and set up civil government – is, all the same, a rational act. There is no need for consensus when the prince himself is rational and governs according to the laws of nature as revealed to him by those qualified to know; at this point the rule of nature, physiocracy, substitutes entirely for the rule of men.

The appeal to history has two dimensions depending on whether it is past or future history from whose authority one is trying to derive the legitimation of power. The recourse to the past installs the force of tradition as a principle of legitimation and is the basis therefore of traditionalistic theories of power according to which the legitimate sovereign is one who has exercised power since time immemorial. The power to command can also be acquired, on the basis of a general principle of law: protracted use over time just as in the acquisition of property or other rights. In his *Reflections on the Revolution in France* (1790) Edmund Burke laid out the theory of historical prescription that justifies the power of monarchs (which gives rise to the claims to legitimacy of dethroned monarchs) against the subversive claims of revolutionaries. While reference to past history constitutes one of the criteria for the legitimation of existing (constituted) power, the reference to future history is one of the criteria for the legitimation of aspirant (constituting) power. The new order which the revolutionary imposes after discarding the old can be justified in so far as it represents a new stage in the course of history, a necessary and inevitable step and an advance on the preceding stage. An order which does not exist yet can only find the source of its legitimacy *post factum*. The conservative has a static view of history: what lasts is good. The revolutionary has a dynamic conception: the good is what corresponds to the predetermined movement of historic progress. Both claim to be in history (representing two historical positions), but the first respects it by accepting it, the second by anticipating it (and perhaps encouraging it).

The debate on criteria of legitimacy does not just have doctrinal value: the problem of legitimacy is closely connected to political obligation because obedience is owed only to the commands of legitimate power. Where the obligation to obey the law ends (obedience can either be active or passive) the right to resistance begins (which can either be active or passive as well). The limits of obedience and the right to resist depend on the criterion of legitimacy assumed. A power which on the grounds of one criterion would be considered legitimate would, on the grounds of another, be considered illegitimate. Of the six criteria listed above some are more favourable to the maintenance of the status quo (that is to say, they are *ex parte principis*); others are more favourable to change, (that is to say, they are *ex parte populi*). On one side is the theocratic principle, the appeal to nature as the source of strength, and tradition; on the other, the democratic principle of consent, the appeal to ideal nature, and historical progress. Whoever looks at resistance movements, in the widest sense of the word, of the world today will not fail to realize the persistence of these criteria; against a despotic government, against a colonial or imperialist power, against a political or economic system seen as unjust and oppressive, the right to resist or revolt is justified by sometimes referring to the oppressed popular will and therefore to the necessity of a new social contract, sometimes to the right of self-determination which is valid not only for individuals but also for groups, and sometimes to the necessity of overthrowing what has been condemned by history and of putting oneself in the flow of historical becoming which proceeds inexorably towards new and more just forms of society.

Legitimacy and effectiveness

The arrival of legal positivism completely reversed the problem of legitimacy. While according to the foregoing theories power must be supported by some ethical justification in order to survive, therefore making legitimacy necessary for effectiveness, in the positivist theory one finds the thesis that only effective power is legitimate: effective in the sense of the principle of effectiveness in international law according to which, in the words of Kelsen who was one of its most authoritative supporters: 'A *de facto* constituted authority is the legitimate government, the coercive order of that government is a legal system, and the community constituted by such a system is a State in the sense of international law insofar as that system is generally effective' (1945). From this point of view legitimacy is purely and simply a matter of fact. This does not mean to say that a legal system, which is legitimate in so far as it is effective and recognized as such by the international order, cannot be subjected to value judgements about its legitimacy which could bring about non-observance of the rules of the system (more or less quickly) and therefore to a process of the delegitimization of the system. It remains the case, however, that on the basis of the principle of effectiveness a regime remains legitimate until its ineffectiveness has reached the point of making probable or foreseeable the effectiveness of an alternative regime.

In the ambit of legal positivism (that is, of a conception in which law is considered law only if made by authorities appointed by the system itself and enforced by other authorities also appointed by the system), the theme of legitimacy has taken another direction: no longer of evaluative criteria but of the reasons for the efficacy from which legitimacy derives. In this area arose the famous Weberian theory of the three forms of legitimate power. Weber posed himself the problem not just of listing the different ways in which every political class has sought to justify its power, but of individuating and describing the historic forms of legitimate power, defined as legitimate power (*Herrschaft*) as distinct from mere force (*Macht*), as the power that succeeds in conditioning the behaviour of the members of a social group, and issuing orders which are habitually obeyed inasmuch as their content is assumed as maxims of action. According to Weber the three pure or ideal types of legitimate power are traditional power, legal–rational power and charismatic power.

In decribing these three types of legitimate power Weber did not mean to present political formulas in Mosca's sense of the word, but instead he meant to understand what were the different reasons why there came to be formed in a given society the stable and enduring relation of obedience/ command which marked out political power. The three types of power represent three different types of motivation: in traditional power the motive for obedience (or, which is the same, the reason why the command is successful) is the belief in the sacredness of the person of the sovereign, a sacredness which belongs to what has lasted for a long time, to what has always existed, and because it has always existed there is no reason to change it; in rational power, the motive for obeying lies in the belief in the rationality of behaviour conforming to the law (that is, to general and abstract norms which institute an impersonal relation between ruler and ruled); in charismatic power, the belief in the extraordinary gifts of the leader. In other words, in the theory of the three types of legitimate power Weber wanted to show what were until then, historically speaking, the real and not the supposed or declared grounds of political power. This does not exclude the possibility of there being a relation between these two approaches and it is difficult to establish where one finishes and the other starts. In the perspective from which one looks not at the evaluative criteria but at the real process of legitimation (and delegitimation) in a given historical context we can locate the recent debate in Niklas Luhmann's theory, which says that in complex societies that have brought to a conclusion the process of positivization of law, legitimacy is the result not of reference to values but of the application of certain procedures (*Legitimität durch Verfahren*) instituted to produce binding decisions: for example, political elections, legislative and judicial procedures. Where the same subjects participate in the proceedings within the limits of the established rules, legitimacy is reckoned as a performance of the system itself (1972).

STATE AND LAW

The constitutive elements of the state

Alongside the problem of the foundation of power the classical doctrine of the state has always been occupied with the problem of the limits of power, a problem generally posed as a problem of the relations between law and power (or law and state).

Ever since lawyers have taken in hand the problem of the state, it has been defined in terms of the three constitutive elements of people, territory and sovereignty (a legal concept *par excellence*, formulated by legalists and universally adopted by writers on public law). To cite an authoritative and current definition, the state is 'a legal arrangement of general ends exercising sovereign power over a given territory to which are subordinated in a necessary manner the subjects belonging to it' (Mortati 1969). In Kelsen's rigorous reduction of the state to the legal system, sovereign power becomes the power to create and apply law (that is, binding norms) in a territory and over a people, a power which derives its validity from the fundamental norm and from the capacity in the last instance to use force, and therefore from the fact of being not only legitimate but also effective (legitimacy and efficacy involve each other); the territory becomes the limit of the geographical validity of the law of the state, in the sense that legal norms originating in sovereign power are only valid within definite boundaries; the people become the limit of the personal validity of the law of the state in the sense that the same legal norms are valid only, except in certain exceptional cases, for given subjects who thereby constitute the citizens of the state. Definitions of this sort shy away from the purpose or the purposes of the state. For Weber,

it is not possible to define a political group – and not even the 'State' – by pointing out the aim of its collective action. There are no aims which political groups have not at some time proposed – from the attempt to provide sustenance to the protection of art; and there is none which they have not all pursued from the guarantee of personal security to law-making. (1908–20)

In Kelsen's terminology, the state (in so far as it is a coercive arrangement) is a technique of social organization: and thus it can be adopted for the most diverse ends. A definition of this type echoes a famous passage of the *Spirit of the Laws* where Montesquieu, wishing to exalt the nation which has political liberty as the aim of its constitution (England), adds: 'All States have in general the same aim of preserving themselves but each one can have a particular aim as well', and he gives some curious examples: 'Expansion was the aim of Rome; war, of Sparta; religion of the Hebrews; trade, of the people of Marseilles, etc.' (1748). Formal definitions and instrumental conceptions of the state go hand-in-hand.

From the point of view of a formal and instrumental definition the necessary and sufficient conditions for the existence of a state are that on a given territory there be formed a power capable of taking decisions and issuing corresponding commands binding on all who inhabit that territory, and effectively executed by the greater part of the addressees in the greater number of cases for which obedience is requested, whatever those decisions might be. This is not to say that state power has no limits. Quite correctly Kelsen takes into account two other types of limit besides the limits of geographical and personal validity which redefine in legal terms the two constitutive terms of territory and people: limits of time, according to which any norm has a validity limited in the time between the moment of its issue (except for cases of retroactive laws) and the time of its abrogation, and the limits of material validity, viz. materials that are not objectively subject to just any regulation. The old saying springs to mind that the English parliament can do anything except change a man into a woman (an example which is, to tell the truth, no longer appropriate), as does Spinoza's assertion that even sovereigns who can do anything they want cannot make a table eat grass. Second, matters that are rendered unassailable by the system itself as, for example, in those regimes in which the protection of some liberty is guaranteed, represented by civil rights in which the state power cannot interfere and a norm although validly issued which violates them can be considered illegitimate by a procedure foreseen by the constitution.

The government of laws

Since antiquity the problem of the relationship between law and power has been posed with this question: 'Which is better, the rule of law or the rule of men?' Plato, distinguishing between good and bad government, says: 'For wherever in a state the law is subservient and impotent, over that state I see ruin impending; but wherever the law is Lord over the magistrates, and the magistrates are servants to the law, there I descry salvation and all the blessings that the Gods bestow on states' (*Laws*, 715d). Aristotle, raising the subject of the different monarchical constitutions, poses the problem of whether it might be 'more convenient to be governed by the best men or by the best laws' (1286a, 9). In favour of the second he pronounces a maxim which was to last: 'The law lacks the passions which necessarily are met with in every human heart' (ibid., 20). The supremacy of the law compared to the individual judgements of the ruler (the Platonic *gubernator*, who rescues his companions from the worst crises, 'does not write laws but offers his skill as law'; see *Politics*, 297a) lies in its generality and its constancy, in not being subjected to the change of passions: this contrast between the passions of human beings and dispassionate law leads to the no less classical *topos* of law being identified with the voice of reason. One of the pivots of medieval political doctrine is the subordination of the prince to the law according to Bracton's aphoristic principle: *Rex non debet esse sub homine, sed sub Deo ed sub lege, quia lex facit regem* (*De legibus et consuetudinibus Angliae*, I, 8, 5). In the English legal tradition the principle of the subordination of the monarch to the law leads to the doctrine of the rule of law, the foundation of the state of law understood in its most restricted sense as the state whose powers are exercised according to laws already laid down. For St Thomas, the *regimen politicum* is distinguished from the *regimen regale* by the fact that the latter is characterized by the *plenaria potestas* of the ruler, while the former occurs '*quando ille qui praeest habet potestatem coarctatam secundum aliquas leges civitatis* (*In octo libros Politicorum Aristotelis expositio*, I, 13).

Naturally such a reply raises a fundamental question: given that laws are generally passed by those who hold power, then where do the laws originate that should be obeyed by the ruler? The Ancients supplied two answers to this question, the first being that, besides the laws passed by the rulers, there exist other laws which do not depend on their will and these are either natural laws deriving from the nature of human beings living in society or laws whose binding force derives from being rooted in some tradition. They are 'unwritten' laws or 'common laws' like those that Antigone obeyed when she violated the tyrant's order, or Socrates when he refused to flee from prison in order to avoid punishment. The second answer is that at the beginning of every good system of laws there is a 'wise man', the great legislator who has given to his people a constitution to which future rulers must carefully conform. This notion of a good legislator who precedes the rulers both temporally and axiologically finds its exemplar in the legend of Lycurgus who, once the state was organized, announced to the people gathered in assembly that he had to leave Sparta to question the oracle and advised them not to change the laws established by him until he got back; but he never came back. Both these paths have been taken in the history of political theory: the rulers who, though being the makers of positive law, are expected to respect laws superior to positive law such as natural law which in medieval thought are also God's laws (*Jus naturale est quod in lege et Evangelio continetur*: the *Decretum Gratiani*, I, i, in Migne, *Patrologia latina,* CLXXXVII, col. 29): or else the laws of the country, the common law of English lawyers which is seen as a law of reason to which even sovereigns are subject. When the idea of natural law becomes exhausted, Rousseau takes up again the myth of the great lawgiver, of the 'extraordinary man' whose function is exceptional because 'it has nothing in common with human authority' and who must establish the conditions of a wise and long-lasting rule (1762). All the original written constitutions, the American just as much as the French, have their origins in the extraordinary historic mission of those that inaugurate with a new body of laws the rule of reason interpreting the laws of nature and transforming them into positive law with a constitution which issues whole out of the mind of the wise.

Internal limits

The recurring idea of the government of laws being superior to the government of men appears to contrast with the principle according to which the *princeps* is *legibus solutus*. Such a principle, derived from a passage in Ulpian (*Digesto,* I, 3, 31), inspired and guided the conduct of sovereigns of the absolute monarchies of continental Europe.

The principle does not mean, as later liberal writers believed (either for polemical reasons or by mistake), that the power of the prince was without limits. The laws to which the principle refers are positive laws: that is laws posed by the will of the sovereign who is not subject to the laws he or she has established because nobody can give a law unto him- or herself. This does not at all exclude that the sovereign might be subject, like all people, to natural and divine laws. Thus Bodin: 'As for natural and divine laws, all the princes of the earth are subjected to them and it is not in their power to transgress them unless they want to make themselves guilty of divine *lèse majesté*' (1576). He and other supporters of absolute monarchy go further: the power of the prince is limited not only by natural and divine laws but also by the fundamental laws of the kingdom: for example, by the law regulating the succession, which are laws handed down, customary laws, and as such positive. The problem of fundamental laws and their binding force is a theme that appears in the treatises of all those jurists who are concerned with fixing by means of clear and certain norms the power of the monarch: they are the norms of that unwritten constitution which governs the relations between rulers and ruled. The ruler who violates natural and divine law becomes a tyrant *ex parte exercitii*; the ruler who violates the fundamental norms is a usurper, a tyrant *ex defectu tituli*. Finally there is a third limit that more than any other distinguishes a proper monarchy from a despotic one: the power of the ruler does not extend to invading the sphere of private law (which is considered a natural right) except in cases of reasonable and justified necessity. Bodin, arguing against the doctrine of the communism of goods proposed by Plato, asserted that 'where there is nothing private then there is nothing public either', and that states were arranged by God 'so that everything that is public goes to the State and to every individual that which is his private property' (Bodin 1576).

The dispute between the supporters of absolute monarchy, such as Bodin and Hobbes, and the supporters of limited or moderate or temperate or regulated monarchy is of a different nature. The latter includes English writers who defend constitutional monarchy by bringing up the ideal model of mixed government, and the French writers who support the resistance of the states against the process of the concentration and centralization of all state power in the hands of the sovereign, interpreting the French monarchy as mixed government. For both, the power of the monarch must be limited not only by the existence of indisputable superior laws but also by the existence of legitimate power-centres – the clergy, the nobility and the cities with their collegial organs – which claim to have the right to decide on determinate matters such as fiscal imposition. It is a question of a limit that stems from the composition and organization of the society and where the estates are victorious (as in England) it is much stronger than the limit set but not imposed by superior laws. On the other hand, even where the resistance of the orders has been broken up, as in France (which is the prototype of absolute states) – while the state of estates survives above all in the small German states – and the monarch governs exclusively through functionaries and commissioners, the process of transformation is never entirely accomplished and never completely obscures the ideal of a monarchy checked by the presence of intermediate bodies, which Montesquieu, looking at England, held to be necessary for his own country also. If the respect for superior laws serves to distinguish the kingdom from the tyranny, the presence of intermediate bodies distinguishes monarchy from despotism. There is no supporter of absolutism that does not know how to distinguish monarchical from tyrannical power on the one hand, and despotic power on the other.

Another phase in the process of the legal limitation of political power is found in the theory and practice of the separation of powers. While the dispute between the estates and the prince concerns the process of the centralization of power that gives rise to the large modern territorial states, the argument about the divisibility or indivisibility of power concerns the parallel process of the concentration of the characteristic functions which belong to whoever holds supreme power in a given territory: the power to make laws, to execute them, and to judge between justice and injustice on their basis. Although the two processes run a parallel course they should be held well distinct because the first has its greatest realization in the division of legislative power between the sovereign and parliament as happened primarily in English constitutional history; the second occurs in the separation and mutual independence of the three powers – legislative, executive and judicial – which has its greatest statement in the written constitution of the United States of America. It is not by chance that, besides the celebrated exposition of the doctrine of the separation of powers made by Montesquieu ('in order that power may not be abused it is necessary that in the arrangement of things power acts as a brake on power'), the clearest and most accomplished exposition of the doctrine is found in certain letters of *The Federalist*, attributed to Madison, where one reads that 'The accumulation of all powers, legislative, executive, and judiciary, in the same hands, whether of one, a few, or many . . . may justly be pronounced the very definition of tyranny' (Hamilton, Jay and Madison 1787–8). Contrary to the then current opinion which the authors of *The Federalist* set out to refute, the separation of powers means not that the three powers must be mutually independent but that it must exclude that whoever possesses all the powers of one given sector also possesses all the powers in another in such a way as to subvert the principle on which a democratic constitution is based; it is necessary to have a certain independence amongst the three powers so that each acts as a constitutional check on the others.

The last battle for the limitation of state power is fought on the terrain of the fundamental rights of the individual and the citizen starting with the personal rights already laid down in King John's Magna Charta (1215) and going on to the various rights of liberty of religion, of political opinion, of the press, of assembly and association which constitute the heart of the Bill of Rights of the American States and of the Declaration of the Rights of Man and the Citizen which emerged from the French Revolution. Whatever might be considered the foundation of the rights of man – God, nature, history or popular consent – they are seen as rights that man possesses *qua* man independently of being affirmed by political power, and consequently political power must not only respect but also protect them. In Kelsen's terminology they constitute limits to the material validity of the state. As such they differ from the other limits considered because they concern the extension of power rather than its quantity. Only their full recognition gives birth to that form of limited state *par excellence* which is the liberal state, and to all later forms which, as well as recognizing other fundamental rights such as political rights and social rights, have not neglected the right of liberty. It is appropriate to call 'constitutionalism' the theory and practice of the limits of power: and therefore constitutionalism finds its fullest expression in the constitution that establishes not just formal but also material limits to political power which are well represented by the barrier which fundamental rights – once recognized and legally protected – raise against the claims and presumptions of the holder of sovereign power to regulate every action of individuals or groups.

External limits

No state is alone. Every state exists alongside others in a society of states. Contemporary states are just like the Greek cities were. Every form of cohabitation – even the state of nature without laws – implies some limits on the conduct of every neighbour: limits of fact which each individual faces concerning every other individual in the state of nature, where everyone has as much right as power (as Spinoza says, 1670, ch. XVI), but no one except God is omnipotent; or legal limits like those posed by law which has regulated since time immemorial the relations between sovereign states, or *ius gentium*, limits deriving from tradition that have become binding (international custom), or reciprocal agreement (international treaties). Sovereignty has two faces, one turned inwards, the other towards the outside. Correspondingly, there are two types of limits: those deriving from the relations between rulers and ruled which are internal limits, and those deriving from the relations between states, and these are external limits. There is a certain degree of correspondence between the two in the sense that the stronger the state and therefore less limited internally, the stronger it is and less limited externally. But there corresponds to the process of internal unification a process of emancipation towards the outside.

The more a state succeeds in binding its own subjects the more it succeeds in becoming independent of other states.

This is what has happened in the formation of the modern state: the process of unification of the diffuse powers that were in conflict amongst themselves that characterized medieval society went hand in hand with the liberation of power thus unified from the two *summae potestates* of the church and the empire. The fewer limits power faced internally – which is to say the more unified it was – the freer, more independent it found itself towards the outside. The formula used by French jurists of the thirteenth century to justify the claims of the sovereign – *rex in regno suo imperator* – expresses the double process well: at the moment in which the king is emperor in his own kingdom, the emperor is no longer king in anyone's kingdom. King and emperor exchange places: what the king gains, the emperor loses (a good example of the theory that sees power as a zero-sum relation). The end of the empire as a power that is a true and genuinely unifying universal state coincides with the rebirth of international law (rebirth, not birth or origin as is often said, because where there are states and independent or self-sufficient powers there has always been recognized the existence of a law to regulate their relations). When Pufendorf (one of the revivers, after Alberico Gentili and Hugo Grotius, of international law) posed the problem of the *status imperii germanici* – that is, if the German empire were still a state in the full sense of the word – he defined it as a *res publica irregularis*, meaning to say that it is no longer a state in the proper sense of the word – and at the same time it is something different from a simple confederation of states (1672, VII, 5, 15). Over a century later, Hegel began his youthful work on the constitution of Germany with the melancholy statement 'Germany [meaning the German Empire] is no longer a State' (1799–1802).

The process of the gradual dissolution of the empire and the formation of territorial and national states was opposed by the reverse process of the gradual unification of small states into larger unions starting with confederations, in which every state preserved its own independence notwithstanding its perpetual union with other states (as originally in Switzerland), until for the first time we have the new and original formation of a federal state with the setting-up of the United States of America (1787). While the dissolution of the empire involves a ceding of power to the new states, the formation of a larger state from the union of smaller states represents a reinforcing of the power of the former over the latter: what they gain in strength vis-à-vis the outside by uniting with others, they lose in internal independence. This was well observed by Montesquieu, to whose authority the authors of *The Federalist* appealed when he eulogized about the 'federal republic' which, 'capable of resisting foreign powers, can maintain its greatness without internal corruption' (1748). Only through federal union can a republic – considered for centuries after the end of the Roman republic the form of government most adapted to small states – become the form of government of a large state like the United States of America. This was understood by Mably when he praised the American Federal Republic in his *Observations sur le gouvernement et les lois des États-Unis d'Amérique* (1784). The suggestive force of the Federal idea – that is, of the model of a large republic formed out of the aggregation of small states – is sufficient to make plausible the idea of a universal federal republic embracing all existing states, making possible again the universalistic ideal of the empire, albeit with a reversed process: that is, no longer descending from high to low but ascending from below to above. The universal republic of confederated states, proposed by Kant in his *Pace Perpetua* (*Zum ewigen Frieden*, 1796), represents a genuine alternative, which can be called democratic on account of its inspiration and its potential development, to the medieval idea of the universal empire. The League of Nations after the First World War and the United Nations after the Second were developments, albeit partial, of this universal republic as opposed to the universal empire: even in the chosen formula of 'United Nations', the states which joined in this new confederation revealed which precedents they were inspired by (the *United* Provinces, the *United* States).

From the point of view of their external relations, the history of European (and not only European) states is a continuous process of decomposition and recomposition, and therefore of the tying and untying of legal limits. The formation of independent and national states in the past two centuries – first in the United States of America, then in Latin America, then again in Europe and finally in the countries of the Third World through the process of decolonization – came about sometimes through the break-up of larger states and sometimes through the regrouping of small states. But regrouping always tends to reinforce internal limits and decomposition to loosen external limits. The present tendency towards the formation of bigger and bigger states or constellations of states (the so-called superpowers) means an increase of the external limits of the states that are absorbed into the larger area (satellite states) and a fall in the external limits of the superstate. If we ever arrive at the formation of a universal state it will be only limited internally and not externally.

THE FORMS OF GOVERNMENT

Classical typologies

In the general theory of the state – even if the line of demarcation is not clear – forms of government are distinguished from types of state. In a typology of the forms of government more attention is paid to the structure of power and to the relations between the different organs which according to the constitution exercise power; in a typology of types of states more attention is paid to relations of class, to the relation between the power system and society, to ideologies and goals, and to historical and sociological characteristics.

There are three classical typologies of the forms of government: Aristotle's, Machiavelli's and Montesquieu's. Going back to Aristotle, in particular to Book III and IV of the *Politics*, one finds the ancestor of the time-honoured classification of constitutions based on the number of rulers: monarchy in the case of one, aristocracy in the case of a few and democracy or the rule of the many along with a doubling up of the corrupt forms of these where monarchy degenerates into tyranny, aristocracy into oligarchy and the *politeia* (which is the name that Aristotle gave to the good form of the rule of the many) into democracy. In *The Prince* Machiavelli reduces these to two, monarchy and republic, the latter including both aristocracy and democracy on the grounds that the essential difference is between the government of one – a physical person – and the government of an assembly, a collective body; the difference between an assembly of patricians and a popular assembly being seen to be less relevant because both, in contrast to the monarchy where the will of one alone is law, must adopt some rule such as the principle of the majority to arrive at the formation of a collective will. Montesquieu returns to a trichotomy of monarchy, republic and despotism, but it is different from Aristotle's. It is different in the sense that it combines the analytic distinction of Machiavelli with that axiological tradition in so far as it defines despotism as the government of one alone but 'without law or restraint': in other words as the degenerate form of monarchy. Moreover, Montesquieu adds another criterion based on the various motivations by which subjects are induced to obey (*ressorts*): honour in the case of the monarchy, virtue in the republic and fear in despotism. This criterion brings to mind the different forms of legitimate power as in Weber. Like Montesquieu, Weber (without being directly influenced) identifies the various types of power by distinguishing between the various possible types of behaviour of the rulers towards the ruled: the difference between them is that Montesquieu was concerned with the functioning of the state machinery and Weber with the capacity of the rulers and their apparatuses to obtain obedience. Compared to the others the novelty of Montesquieu's typology depends on the introduction of the category of despotism made necessary by the exigency of making a wider space for the oriental world, for which the category of despotism had been designed by the ancients.

In the nineteenth century Montesquieu's typology had the good luck to be taken up by Hegel, who adopted it to outline the historic development of humanity which passed from a primitive phase of despotism, corresponding to the birth of the great oriental states, through the epoch of the republics, democratic in Greece and aristocratic in Rome, and finishing with the Christian–Germanic monarchies which characterized the modern age. The traditional typology, notwithstanding later corrections and innovations, never lost its prestige and was taken up again in the treatises on public law, if not as the point of arrival then as the obligatory point of departure of every discussion of the theme (for example, in Schmitt's *Verfassungslehre*, 1928).

Kelsen's is the only interesting innovation. Starting from the definition of the state as a legal system, it criticized the Aristotelian typology as superficial for being based on an extrinsic element such as number, and claimed that the only rigorous way to distinguish between forms of government consisted in identifying the ways in which a constitution regulates the production of the legal system. There are two and not three modes: the legal system can be created (and continually modified) either from the top or from the bottom: from the top when the addressees of the norms do not participate in their creation and from the bottom when they do. Kelsen, drawing on the Kantian distinction between autonomous and heteronomous norms, calls the first form of norm production heteronomous and the second autonomous. Corresponding to these two forms of production are two pure or ideal forms of government: autocracy and democracy. It was seen previously how

Machiavelli had reduced the classical forms of government to two. The Machiavellian typology is a result of uniting aristocracy and democracy in the form of the republic while the Kelsenian is a result of uniting monarchy and aristocracy into autocracy. Naturally, Kelsen takes care to point out that autocracy and democracy are pure forms and no existing state corresponds perfectly to either of the two definitions. Only ideological expressions of the one or the other can correspond exactly: when Hegel defines Oriental despotism as a regime in which only one person (the despot) is free, he is giving a correct definition of the autocratic form of government in Kelsen's sense; in the same way, Rousseau's republic, where the principle of a self-ruling people is realized through the general will, corresponds to the democratic form.

Monarchy and republic

The most time-honoured distinction, even if in our day somewhat attenuated, is the Machiavellian distinction between monarchy and republic. Increasingly attenuated because, with the fall of most monarchical governments after the First and Second World Wars it has been less relevant to historical reality. In the last 50 years the traditional relations between monarchy and republic have been completely reversed: the large modern territorial state is born, grows and consolidates itself as monarchical state; it is the *regnum* contrasted not to the *res publica* but to the *civitas*. The great political writers, who with their theorizing sought to give body to a genuine doctrine of the state, were for the most part supporters of monarchy – from Bodin to Hobbes, from Vico to Montesquieu, from Kant to Hegel. In writers such as Vico, Montesquieu and Hegel who construct their philosophy of history and their theory of progress on the replacement of one form of government by another, the monarchy stands for the form of government of the moderns, the republic that of the ancients or in the modern age the form of government suitable for small states alone. The United States of America, the first republic after Rome to be founded on a large territory, gave itself a constitution seen as the image and likeness of a monarchical constitution in which the head of state is not hereditary but elected. Also, for another conceptual and not historical reason, the distinction between monarchy and republic gradually loses all relevance, and it loses it because it loses its original meaning. Originally a monarchy was the government of one alone, and a republic, in the Machiavellian sense of the word, the government of many (and more precisely of an assembly). Now, little by little, starting with the British case, as the weight of power started to shift from the monarch to parliament, the monarchy became first constitutional and then parliamentary and was transformed into a form of government quite different from the one for which the word was coined and used for centuries: it is a mixed form, half monarchy and half republic. It is not by chance that Hegel saw in the constitutional monarchy of his own day the new incarnation of the mixed government of the ancients. At this point the distinction between monarchy and republic became so evanescent that the treatises of constitutional law that still adopted it were hard-pushed to find a convincing criterion of distinction between one and the other. When Machiavelli wrote that every state was either a principality or a republic, he was making an assertion that corresponded perfectly to the reality of this time and he was distinguishing between things that were really different: the monarchy of France from the Venetian Republic. The same distinction repeated today would force reality into an inadequate if not actually distorting framework because it would distinguish things that are not easily distinguishable: the British monarchy from the Italian Republic, for example.

Once governments characterized by the separation between the power of government, strictly speaking, and legislative power became more widespread, the only adequate criterion of distinction was one which highlighted the different relations between the two powers independent of the fact that the holder of one of the two powers might either be a monarch or the president of a republic. Kant had already called republican that form of government where the principle of the separation of powers operated even if the holder of executive power was a monarch. In this manner 'republic' acquired a new meaning: it no longer means a state, generally speaking, or even government by assembly contrasted with government by one individual, but instead a form of government possessing a certain internal structure compatible even with the existence of a monarch. The different relation between the two forms constituted the criterion for the distinction between presidential and parliamentary government; in the first a clean-cut separation between the power of government and the power of making laws operates, a separation which is based on the direct election of a president of the republic (who is also the head of government and to whom, rather than the parliament, the components of government are responsible); in the second, rather than a separation, there is a network of reciprocal powers between government and parliament, based on the distinction between the head of state and the head of government, on the indirect election of the head of state by parliament, and on the responsibility of the government to parliament which is expressed in a vote of confidence (or no confidence). Between these two pure forms there are many intermediate ones: it is enough to think of the Fifth French Republic, established in 1958, a presidential republic *sui generis* which kept separate the offices of the president of the council and president of the republic. But there is no need to describe them in detail because the distinction between presidential government and parliamentary government, on account of being purely formal and constructed on mechanisms with which the system of constitutional powers should function rather than on their effective functioning, was little by little supplanted by typologies paying more attention to real, if informal, powers.

The greater quantity of real political power, even if not

formally recognized, has been accumulated in modern democracies and states by political parties as an effect both of the process of democratization which made necessary the aggregation of demands originating in civil society, and of the formation of mass society where only parties, or even one party alone, can succeed in expressing one will and one political programme. Today no typology can ignore the party system: that is, the way in which the political forces, from which government draws its life, are disposed and arranged. The party system influences the formal constitution to the point of changing its structure. Duverger had already observed how the party system particularly influences the separation of powers. A perfect two-party system, such as the British one (which has two main parties which tend to alternate in government and where generally the leader of a party becomes the head of government if that party wins the election), brings the parliamentary form of government closer to the presidential in that the prime minister is elected, albeit indirectly, by the citizens who choose a prime minister indirectly at the same time as they choose a party. A one-party system, no matter what the formal constitution says, gives rise to a form of government in which the greatest power is concentrated in the committee of the party (and its secretary) to the detriment of all the collegial and popular organs provided for in the constitution; so much so that the traditional distinction between despotism and democracy coincides with the distinction between one-party and more-than-one-party systems (whether two- or multi-party systems). There are also differences between two-party and multi-party systems depending on whether the multi-party system is polarized (with two extreme anti-system parties on the right and left) or not: that is to say, with many pro-system parties. Here too there are many variations and it is not possible (and perhaps not especially useful in this context) to take account of them all.

To show how the classic distinction of forms of government became overlaid by the distinction between party systems we will limit ourselves to citing the typology proposed by a constitutionalist aware of the necessity of not seeing legal problems in a rigidly formalistic way: rigid two-party parliamentary government, moderate multi-party parliamentary government, extreme multi-party parliamentary government and presidential government (Elia 1970, p. 642) which could be respectively exemplified by British parliamentary government, by the governments of the so-called 'small democracies' except for Switzerland (such as the Scandinavian, Dutch and Belgian monarchies and the Austrian Republic), by the Italian Republic and by the government of the United States. Switzerland is unique with its directorial form of government characterized by a federal council elected by parliament but not responsible to it and made up of seven members who remain in charge for four years, of which each one in turn is president for a year.

Other typologies

If one takes as the distinguishing element not the party but the political class understood, according to Gaetano Mosca, as the group of persons who effectively wield political power or, according to the expression introduced and made popular by Wright Mills, as the power elite, it is possible to construct new typologies different from both traditional ones and those current in public law. Once it is admitted, as Mosca asserts, that the government in every political system belongs to a minority, the forms of government can no longer be distinguished on the basis of the old criterion of the number of governors; from this point of view all governments are oligarchies. However, that does not imply that one may not be distinguished from another. Accepting the principle of the necessity of a political class, the various forms of government can be distinguished on the basis of either the formation or organization of the political class. Concerning formation Mosca distinguished between open and closed classes, and concerning organization between autocratic classes where power comes from the top and democratic classes where power comes from below. The

combination of the two distinctions generates four forms
of government: aristocratic in formation and democratic in
organization, and so on. According to the notion of a power
elite, however, there is Schumpeter's distinction between
democratic governments, in which there is more than
one elite competing amongst themselves for access to
government, and autocratic governments in which one elite
possesses the monopoly of government.

If the political system rather than the political class is
taken as the point of reference (the political system
understood as the ensemble of interdependent relations
between the various elements which together contribute to
the performance of the functions of conflict mediation, of
group cohesion and of defence from other groups), then it
is possible to construct other typologies. One of the most
noted, proposed by Almond and Powell (1966), distinguishes
between sub-systems by using two criteria: the differentiation of roles and the autonomy of political systems.
Putting together the two characteristics on a scale going
from high to low, four ideal types of political system can
be picked out: (a) low differentiation of roles and low
autonomy of sub-systems, as in primitive societies; (b) low
differentiation of roles along with high autonomy of sub-
systems, as in feudal societies; (c) high autonomy of sub-
systems and low differentiation of roles, as in the large
monarchies born of the dissolution of feudal societies; (d)
high differentiation of roles and high autonomy of sub-
systems, as in modern democratic states.

Mixed government

Nothing demonstrates the vitality of traditional typologies
more than the continuity of the theory of mixed governments, according to which the best forms of government
result from a combination of the two or three (depending
on the typology) forms of pure government. In the *Laws*
Plato, after declaring that monarchies and democracies are
the precursors of all other forms of government, adds: 'the

participation of both is obligatory and necessary if there is to be liberty and intelligent agreement' (693d). Aristotle cites the opinion which says that 'the best constitution must be a combination of all constitutions', and thus praises the Spartan constitution because its ruling authority constitutes the monarchical element, the oligarchic element is represented by the 'elders' and the democratic element by the 'ephors' (magistrates) in so far as they come from the people (*Politics*, 1265b, 35). When he puts forward his own theory of governmental forms he describes the *politeia*, the good form of popular government, as 'a mixture of oligarchy and democracy' (1293f, 35). The most accomplished theory of mixed government is that laid out by Polybius in the *Histories*, where his account of the events of the Second Punic War are interrupted by an exposition of the Roman constitution interpreted as the most authoritative example of mixed government: the consuls represent the monarchical principle, the senate the oligarchical element and the *comitia* of the people the democratic one. According to Polybius the reason why mixed government is superior to all others lies in the fact that 'each organ can either obstruct or collaborate with the others' and 'no part exceeds its competence and goes over the limit' (VI, 18): an argument which anticipated by centuries the celebrated theory of the balance of powers which was to be one of the principal arguments of the supporters of constitutional monarchy against the defenders of absolute monarchy. Cicero, too, in *De re publica* (I, 29, 45) asserts that of all the forms of government the best is the *moderatum et permixtum*. In the modern age the doctrine of mixed government is used to highlight the excellence of the British constitution as opposed to the French monarchy, and in general any government which one wants to commend: the republic of Venice or the republic of Florence have in turn been described as mixed governments by those who propose one or the other as the ideal form of government, or at least as the form to imitate above all others.

Theorists of absolutism (that is, of a state which neither

knows nor recognizes intermediate elements), such as Bodin and Hobbes, criticize the doctrine of mixed government for the same reason that its supporters advance it: the distribution of sovereign power between different and distinct organs causes the worst disadvantage that can affect a state: instability; exactly the same instability that Polybius considered as common among pure forms which were continually replacing each other, and which only a combination of the three forms could prevent.

Through Montesquieu's idealization of the English monarchy, which he believed realized the principle of the separation of powers – although with a shift in the real meaning of the doctrine in so far as the mixture of the three forms of government is one thing and the separation of powers is another – constitutional monarchy became the universal model of the state for at least a century after the French Revolution. It is significant that Hegel, after having highlighted the inadequacy of the three ancient forms for an understanding of modern monarchy, affirmed that 'they are downgraded to moments of constitutional monarchy: the monarch is one; the few participate in the governing power and the majority is present in the legislative power' (1821). Again, after the First World War, one of the greatest periods of constitutional transformations known in history, Carl Schmitt claimed that the constitutions of the modern bourgeois state were mixed because different elements and principles (democratic, monarchical and aristocratic) were united and mixed in them thereby confirming an ancient tradition according to which the ideal public arrangement rested on a union and mixture (*Verbindung und Mischung*) of different political principles (1928). The theory of mixed government occupied an important position in the work of Gaetano Mosca who, in the conclusion to his *Storia delle dottrine politiche* (*History of Political Doctrines*, 1933) where he gives the final version of his theory of the forms of government, writes that the objective study of history shows that the best regimes (and by 'best regimes' he means those that last longest: once again the value of a constitution resides in its stability) are mixed governments; by 'mixed government' he means not just those forms where the different principles are adopted but also where religious power is separate from secular power and economic power from political power.

Historical forms

There are so many elements to take into account when distinguishing between forms of state – especially the relations between political organization and society or else the different ends pursued by organized political power in different historical epochs and different societies – and the resulting typologies of the forms of state are so numerous that it would be difficult and perhaps useless to attempt their complete exposition. To bring a little order into such rich and controversial material two main criteria can be used to distinguish between different state forms: a historical criterion and a criterion taking account of the greater or lesser expansion of the state with respect to society (a criterion that includes those based on different ideologies).

On the basis of the historical criterion, the typology that is most widespread and accepted amongst historians of institutions proposes the following sequence: feudal state, corporate state (involving the various estates), absolute state, representative state. The presence of a corporate state between the feudal state and the absolute state goes back to Otto von Gierke and Max Weber, and after Weber was taken up mostly by German historians of institutions. In Mosca's *Elementi di scienza politica* (1896), two ideal types of the state stand out, the feudal one on the one hand characterized by the accumulative exercise of the different directive functions by the same people and the fragmentation of central power into small social aggregates and the bureaucratic state, on the other characterized by a progressive centralization and at the same time progressive specialization of the functions of government. By a corporate state (*Ständestaat*) [in the original Italian *Stato di ceto*, which means literally 'class-' or 'rank state' – translator's note] is meant a political system where collegial organs have been formed – the *Stände* or estates – which bring together people of the same social position, enjoying rights and privileges which count against the holder of sovereign power through deliberative asssemblies such as parliaments. To Otto Hinze is chiefly owed the distinction between states with two assemblies such as Britain, where the House of Lords includes the clergy and the nobility and the House of Commons the bourgeoisie, and corporate states, such as France, with three distinct bodies, respectively the clergy, the nobility and the bourgeoisie.

However, the formation of institutions representative of category-interests acting to counterbalance the power of the prince is common to all European states. The dispute between the estates and the prince, especially about establishing who has the right to impose taxes, constitutes a large part of the history and development of the modern state in the passage from the extensive type to the intensive type of political management (another of Hinze's distinctions) between the end of the medieval and the start of the modern age. But even where the corporate state was not directly transformed into a parliamentary state (as in Britain) or did not survive the French Revolution and after as in the German states (Hegel's constitutional monarch is an idealization of it), with the exception of Prussia, it is never easy to trace a clear line of demarcation between the corporate state and absolute monarchy. No monarchy becomes so absolute, as has more than once been observed, as to suppress every form of intermediate power (the absolute state is not a totalitarian state). The idea of a moderate monarchy has a long life. The supporters of a *reglée* monarchy, like Claude de Seysell at the start of the sixteenth century, were representative of the idea of a monarchy controlled by the power of the estates. Thus in

Montesquieu's theory of the forms of government, monarchy is distinct from despotism because monarchical power is counterbalanced by intermediate bodies. For Hegel, too, while the despot exercises power without intermediaries, 'he cannot personally exercise all the powers of government but entrusts some part of the exercise of particular powers to the colleges or classes of the kingdom' (1808–12). As an intermediate form between the feudal state and the absolute state, the corporate state is distinguished first by a gradual institutionalization of counterbalancing powers and also by the transformation of the person-to-person relations of the feudal system into relations between institutions (on the one side the assemblies of the estates and, on the other, the monarchs with their apparatus of officials which, getting the upper hand, gave rise to the bureaucratic state characteristic of the absolute monarchy); second, by the presence of counterbalancing powers in continual conflict amongst themselves which the advent of the absolute monarchy tended to suppress.

The formation of the absolute state came about through parallel processes of the concentration and centralization of power over a given territory: by concentration is meant the process whereby the powers through which sovereignty is exercised, the power to dictate valid laws for the entire society (to the point that customs are considered valid by means of a legal fiction which presumes that they are tolerated by the monarch as long as he or she has not expressly abrogated them), the power of jurisdiction, the exclusive power to use internal and external force, and finally the power to impose tribute, are attributed *de jure* to the sovereign by the lawyers and exercised *de facto* by the monarch and by functionaries directly dependent on him or her. By centralization is meant the process of the elimination or removal of the authority of lesser legal entities such as the city, the corporation and specialized associations which no longer survive as primary and autonomous systems but as arrangements derived from the authorization or tolerance of the central power. In a usually neglected chapter of Hobbes's

Leviathan (1651) dedicated to partial societies one reads that, of regular systems, the only ones that are absolute and independent – that is, not subject to anyone but their representatives – are states; all the rest, from the cities to commercial societies, are dependent on (that is to say, subordinate to) sovereign power, and legitimate only in so far as recognized by it.

The representative state

With the advent of the representative state, first as a constitutional and then as a parliamentary monarchy in England after the Great Rebellion, and in the rest of Europe after the French Revolution, and in the form of a presidential republic in the United States of America after the revolt of the 13 colonies, the fourth phase of the transformation of the state began, and still continues. While in England the representative state was born almost without problems of continuity from the feudal state and the corporate state through the civil war and the 'Glorious Revolution' of 1688, in continental Europe it was born out of the ruins of absolute monarchy. Like the corporate state, the representative state was the result of a compromise between the power of the prince whose principle of legitimacy was tradition, and the power of the representative of the people (where by people is meant, at least to begin with, the bourgeois class) whose principle of legitimacy is agreement. The difference between the corporate state and the representative state lies in the fact that representation by category or corporation (nowadays one would say the representation of interests) is substituted by the representation of individuals (at one time just the proprietors) whose political rights are recognized. Between the corporate state and the absolute state on the one hand and the representative state on the other, whose sovereign subjects are no longer princes invested by God or the people as an undifferentiated and collective subject (a mere legal fiction of Roman and medieval jurists), there is the discovery and affirmation of the natural rights of the individual, of the rights that each individual has by nature and that, precisely because they are innate and not acquired, can be made to count against the state by the individual even having recourse to the extreme .remedy of civil disobedience and resistance. The recognition of the rights of individuals and citizens, at the beginning only in a doctrinal manner by natural lawyers and then later practically and politically in the first declarations of rights, represents a genuine Copernican revolution in the evolution of the relationship between rulers and ruled; the state no longer considered *ex parte principis* but *ex parte populi*. The individual is not for the state but the state for the individual. The parts are prior to the whole and not the whole prior to the parts (as in Aristotle and Hegel). The ethical presupposition of the representation of individuals *qua* individuals is the natural equality of human beings. Every person counts as that person and not as a result of belonging to this or that particular group.

That the natural equality of individuals might have been the ethical postulate of representative democracies (called atomistic by its detractors) does not mean that representative states recognized this from the start. The development of the representative state coincides with successive phases of enlargement of political rights right down to the recognition of universal male and female suffrage. Amongst other things this made organized parties necessary and profoundly altered the structure of the representative state to the point of bringing about a fundamental change in the system of representation itself (which is no longer representation by single individuals but is filtered through powerful associations that organize elections and receive a blank proxy from the electorate). While in a representative political system with restricted suffrage it is individuals who elect individuals (especially in elections conducted with single-member constituencies) and parties form inside parliament, in a representative political system with universal suffrage parties develop outside parliament and the electorate chooses a party rather than a person (especially with a proportional system). This alteration of the system of representation has transformed the representative state into a state of parties in which, like the corporate state, the relevant political actors are no longer individuals but organized groups, although no longer organized on the basis of category of corporate interests but of class or more general interests. Max Weber had already noticed that, where group interests confront each other, the normal procedure for reaching collective decisions is compromise between the parties and not majority rule (which is the golden rule for collective decisions in bodies constituted by subjects considered at least partially equal). Weber made this observation about the corporate state. Now everyone can see how valid this description is for actual party systems in which collective decisions are the fruit of negotiation and agreements between groups which represent social forces (unions) and political forces (parties) rather than an assembly where majority voting operates. These votes take place, in fact, so as to adhere to the constitutional principle of the modern representative state, which says that individuals and not groups are politically relevant (and where there are organs capable of taking binding decisions the procedure for the formation of the collective will is majority rule); but they end up possessing the purely formal value of ratifying decisions reached in other places by the process of negotiation.

On a game-theory basis, a majority decision is the outcome of a zero-sum game; a decision reached through an agreement between parties is the outcome of a positive sum game. In the first, what the majority wins the minority loses; in the second both parts gain something (compromise is only possible when the both partners believe, looking at the pros and cons, that each has something to gain). In our pluralist societies composed of large organized groups in conflict amongst themselves, the negotiation procedure serves to keep the social system in balance, more than majority rule which, by dividing contestants into winners and losers, allows the reweighting of the system only when the minority becomes in its turn the majority.

Socialist states

The last phase of the historical sequence just described by no means exhausts the phenomenon of existing forms of the state. In fact, the majority of states in today's international community are not included, although more for *de facto* than *de jure* reasons. Military dictatorships, despotic states governed by leaders responsible to no one, recently-formed states dominated by restricted oligarchies that are not democratically controlled; all these render homage to representative democracy and justify their own power as temporarily necessary in order to restore order or get over a transitory period of anarchy; as with a provisional government in a state of emergency and therefore not as a refutation of the democratic system but as its temporary suspension until the return of normality, or as the imperfect application of principles sanctioned by a solemnly approved constitution but too rapidly taken up by a ruling class formed in the West and imposed on a country with no tradition of self-government and of political contest regulated by the recognition of civil rights. The representative state that formed in Europe over the past 300 years is still today the ideal model for written constitutions that have been affirmed in the last decade, even where they have been suspended or badly applied (the bad application of a constitution is not especially a vice of the Third World).

The states which are not included even in principle are the socialist states, beginning with the pioneer state, the Soviet Union. But what form of state they represent is not easy to say, the gap being too large between official proclamations of the constitution and the facts, between the formal and the substantive constitutions. There is no commonly accepted definition among lawyers and political scientists of the form of state of the Soviet Union after the dictatorship of the proletariat, which was at least an historically and doctrinally relevant formula. The definition of the republic of councils becomes increasingly unacceptable and remains in name alone as a reminder of a now remote origin.

Lacking an official definition current characterizations are, for the most part, attempts to isolate the predominant element or elements. To point out some of them: in the wake of Weber's analysis of the process of formal rationalization (not always accompanied by the process of substantive rationalization) that characterizes the modern state and has as a consequence the growth of depersonalized bureaucratic apparatuses and the transformation of the traditional state into the legal–rational state, and from Weber's own catastrophic vision of the ineluctable coming of a bureaucratic state in a collectivized world, one of the most common interpretations of the Soviet state adopted during the years of Stalin's incontestable domination, authoritatively confirmed by Trockij, sees it as a bureaucratic state dominated by an oligarchy which renews itself by cooption.

However, a bureaucracy administers and does not govern. The interpretation of the Soviet state as a bureaucratic state must be weighed against the claim that in a world of party states that have come about through mass suffrage and mass society, the essential difference between representative democracies and the socialist states lies in the contrast between multi-party systems and one-party systems (like the Soviet Union in principle and other popular democracies in fact). The domination of one party introduces into the political system the monocratic principle of monarchical government of the past, and perhaps constitutes the genuine characteristic element of socialist states of direct or indirect Leninist inspiration, compared with the polyarchic systems of Western democracies. The immovable motor of the system is the party, this collective prince which is the holder of political and ideological power and consequently recognizes no distinction between *regnum* and *sacerdotium*;

a sovereign whose legitimacy derives from considering itself as the only authentic interpreter of doctrine (a principle of legitimacy more appropriate to churches than to states and which, in fact, was not amongst the principles discussed above).

The analysis of states with one all-pervading and omnipotent party has given rise to the image of the total or totalitarian state which, besides the historically incorrect polemical arguments equating fascist and communist states, offers the most faithful representation of a political organization in which the distinct line of demarcation between state and church has disappeared on the one hand (where by 'church' is meant not just the sphere of religious life but also contemplative life in the classical sense of the term and spiritual life in the modern and secular sense) and between state and society on the other (where 'civil society' has the Marxist sense of economic relations); and which therefore extends its control over all human behaviour, leaving no interstices where individual and group initiatives can legitimately develop. Finally, the definition of the Soviet state as oriental despotism (Wittfogel) should not be forgotten, although it is grounded on a historical reconstruction rather than a structural analysis. It should be remembered that despotism has always been understood, at least since Aristotle onwards, as that form of government in which rulers rule over their subjects like owners over their slaves or, in Machiavelli's graphic expression, 'one a prince and all the rest slaves' as in Turkey (1513).

State and non-state

This reference to the category of the totalitarian and its definition allows us to pass on to the second criterion of classification of forms of states mentioned on p. 111. In totalitarian states all society is resolved in the state, in the organization of political power that unites in itself ideological and economic power. There is no space for the non-state. The totalitarian state represents an extreme case since even the state in its widest meaning (including the Greek *polis*) always found itself confronted with the non-state in both the religious sphere (in the largest sense of the word) and the economic sphere. Even in the ideal Aristotelian model, in which people are political animals, the economic sphere breaks down into the 'household management' and exchange relations and does not belong to the state; the contemplative life whose superiority Aristotle claimed over the active life belongs to the wise. The Hobbesian state, although subordinating church to state and giving itself the power to prohibit seditious theories and claiming the monopoly of ideological power, leaves the fullest economic liberty to its subjects. In the opposite way Hegel's ethical state, often interpreted as the all-state, is the final moment of objective spirit beyond which there is absolute spirit which includes the highest expressions of spiritual life: art, religion and philosophy. The presence of the non-state in both or either of its two forms has always constituted a limit to the expansion of the state in fact and in principle, in objective reality and in the speculations of political writers. This boundary varies from state to state; the highlighting of these variations constitutes therefore a potentially useful criterion for distinguishing between historical forms of the state. However, one should not confuse the limit the state is faced with, from the more or less strong presence of the non-state, with the legal limits of political power discussed in the section on state and law. These are the limits *of* political power; in the next two paragraphs are found the limits *to* political power.

With the advent of Christianity as a universal religion crossing the boundaries of single states, the problems of the relations between religious society and political society became a permanent problem of European history. In the classical world the non-state in, for example, the universal republic of the Stoics is an ideal of life and not an institution, whereas with the diffusion of Christianity the non-state becomes an institution with which the state has to deal continually, a genuine power that proclaims from the start

its supremacy over terrestrial power with the principle
imperator intra ecclesiam, non supra ecclesiam (St Ambrose,
Sermo contra Auxentium, 36). According to the Gelasian
doctrine (named after Pope Gelasio I): *Duo sunt quibus
principaliter mundus hic regitur: auctoritas sacrata pontificum
et regalis potestas* (*Epistulae*, XII, 2). The *potestas regalis*,
too, gets its real investiture from God (*nulla potestas nisi a
Deo*, St Paul, Letter to the Romans, 13:1), but its purpose
in this world is peace on earth, whether internal or external,
and as such is subordinate to the aim of *auctoritas sacrata
pontificum*, which is the preaching and realization of a
doctrine of salvation. It is up to the prince to eradicate evil
and exterminate heretics, but it is the privilege of the church
to establish what is good and what is evil, who is a heretic
and who not.

For our own purposes it is interesting to note that, in a
doctrine of the primacy of non-state, the state turns into
the possession and legitimate exercise of coercive power, a
merely instrumental power in that its services are indispensable but by their nature of an inferior rank to a power
ordained from on high. This annotation is interesting
because the same instrumental representation of the state
occurs when the non-state that makes these claims of
superiority against the state is the bourgeois civil society.
In feudal society political and economic power were
inseparable from each other and, moreover, the *imperium*
could not exist without some form of *dominium* (*dominium
eminens* at least): a confusion that remained until a
specifically patrimonial right such as hereditary succession
continued to be valid not just for goods but also for the
transmission of political power and state functions. With
the formation of the bourgeois class which fought against
feudal bonds for its own emancipation, civil society as a
realm of economic relations obeying natural laws superior
to positive law (according to the Physiocratic doctrine) or
regulated by a superior rationality (the market or Smith's
invisible hand) claimed to detach itself from the mortal
embrace of the state: economic power becomes clearly

distinct from political power and, at the end of this processs, the non-state affirmed itself as superior to the state both in the classical economic doctrine and Marxist doctrine albeit with opposed values. The chief consequence of the primacy of the non-state over the state is once again a merely instrumental notion of the state, and its reduction to the element that characterizes it: coercive power, whose exercise in the service of the holders of economic power should be to guarantee the autonomous development of civil society and transform the state into a genuine 'secular arm' of the dominant economic class.

Maximalist and minimalist state

The Christian state and the bourgeois state are two extreme cases. They are the configurations of the state, expressing the point of view of the non-state, to which reality does not always correspond. From the point of view of the state, relations with the non-state vary according to the greater or lesser expansion of the former over the latter. From this perspective as well, two ideal types can be distinguished: the state that takes on tasks which the non-state, in its superiority, claims for itself; and the indifferent or neutral state.

In the religious sphere these two approaches give rise to the two images of the confessional state and the lay state; in the economic sphere the interventionist state, which takes on various historical forms (the most persistent of which is the *Wohlfart Staat* of the eighteenth century reborn in the contemporary Welfare State), and the abstentionist state. Like the confessional state which, in assuming a given religion as the state religion, busies itself with the religious behaviour of its subjects and to this end controls their external acts, opinions and writings, preventing any demonstration of dissent and persecuting dissidents, the state that considers its own the manner in which economic relations take place, takes on a given economic doctrine (mercantalism in the eighteenth century and Keynesianism in the last 50 years), claims for itself the overall right of regulating the production of goods or the distribution of riches, facilitates some activities and impedes others and stamps its character on the economic activity of the country. Both the confessional state and the interventionist state can be seen in the eighteenth-century eudemonic state, which had as its goal the happiness of its subjects (happiness being understood as the possibility of pursuing, besides the greatest earthly goods, the other-worldly good that only true religion can provide). The liberal state, diametrically opposed to the eudemonic state, is both lay as regards the religious sphere and abstentionist as regards the economic sphere (it is not by accident that it is often described in religious terms: agnostic). It is also defined as the state of law (according to one of the many meanings of this expression), having no external aims that originate in the non-state, and no purpose other than legally guaranteeing the most autonomous development of the two bordering spheres; in other words, the widest possible expression of religious liberty and the widest possible expansion of economic liberty.

The process of secularization, or the emancipation of the state from religious affairs, and the process of liberalization, or the emancipation of the state from economic affairs, advanced hand-in-hand in the modern age. Both are the effect of a crisis in the paternalistic conception of power and of the Enlightenment which has been defined since Kant as the coming of age of man. Emphatically and diametrically opposed to the Welfare State is the custodian or 'gendarme' state. This double process can be described as the process on the part of the state of the demonopolization of ideological power on the one side, and the demonopolization of economic power on the other. The monopoly of violence remains with the state and will stay with it as long as it remains a state, ensuring the free circulation of ideas (and therefore the end of all orthodoxy) and the free circulation of goods (and therefore the end of every form of protectionism). In reality, however, the process was not so linear as liberals of the last century believed. The confessional state reappeared in the form of the doctrinal state which tolerates one doctrine alone (for example, Marxist-Leninism), giving rise again to the distinction between the orthodox and the heretical (or renegades, which is a typical expression of religious language), and which emerges moreover in countries where secularization never took place (such as Islamic states) or was imposed by force. The state which takes on itself the task of directing the economy has reappeared as the socialist state and, even if in a blander form with regard to the distributive system alone and not the productive one, in the so-called *Sozialstaat* – social state – or state of justice proposed by social-democratic parties.

Two interpretations can be given to this depending on whether they judge favourably or not the changes wrought in the liberal state (internally liberal even if protectionist towards the outside): that called by well-disposed interpreters the state of social justice which corrects some of the distortions of the capitalist state for the benefit of the less advantaged classes is, for the left-wing critics who have not renounced the ideal of socialism or communism, 'the state of capital', or, in the less recent expression, the 'state of organised capitalism' (Hilferding); a system of power which the capitalist system makes use of to survive and to prosper, the pre-condition of 'exploitation' in a society where the strength of the antagonists (the worker's movement) has grown enormously thanks to democratic power structures. To judge from the actual state of the debate, left-wing criticism has had the effect not of opening up the way to a deeper transformation of the state – disparagingly called 'assistential' – into a state of greater socialist content, but of reawakening neo-liberal nostalgia and hope.

THE END OF THE STATE

The positive conception of the state

Engels's thesis is well known: the state, just as it had an origin, will also have an end and it will finish when the causes that produced it disappear. Just as much as the origin of the state the end of the state is a recurring theme. However, it is above all necessary to distinguish the problem of the end of the state from the problem of the crisis of the state, about which so much has been said in recent times with reference either to the theme of growing intricacy and consequent ungovernability of complex society, or to the phenomenon of diffuse power which makes it increasingly difficult to bring about the decisional unity that has characterized the state since its birth. By the crisis is meant, by conservative writers, a crisis of the democratic state unable to deal with the demands from civil society which have been provoked by itself; by socialist or Marxist writers, a crisis of the capitalist state which no longer succeeds in controlling the power of competing interest groups. The crisis of the state means for both the crisis of a particular sort of state and not the end of the state. Proof of this lies in the return to the agenda of the new 'social contract' in order to give life to a new form of state, different from both the capitalist or unjust state and the socialist or unfree state.

The theme of the end of the state is closely connected to positive and negative value judgements that have been made and that continue to be made on this maximum concentration of power's having the right of life and death over individuals who rely on it or who suffer it passively. The entire history of political thought is shot through by the opposition between positive and negative conceptions of the state. The negative conception is a necessary but not sufficient condition of the ideal of the end of the state. Whoever makes a positive judgement on the state, whoever believes that the state might be, if not the greatest good, at least an institution favourable to the development of human faculties, to civil progress, *civil society* in the eighteenth-century use of the term, will tend not to celebrate the end of the state but applaud the gradual extension of state institutions (*in primis*, the monopoly of violence as long as it is controlled by democratic institutions) until a universal state is formed. In fact the Utopia of the universal state has had no fewer supporters than the end of the state.

The positive conception of the state has as its ancestor according to a well-established tradition the *eu zen* (the *bonum vivere*) of Aristotle taken up by scholastic philosophy following the translation into Latin of the *Politics* (in the second half of the thirteenth century): the *polis* exists to 'make a happy life possible' (*Politics*, 1252b, 30). But it culminates in the rational conception of the state that goes from Hobbes through Spinoza and Rousseau to Hegel: rational, because it is dominated by the idea that outside the state there is a world of unleashed passions or antagonistic and irreconcilable interests, and individuals can only realize their true lives as people of reason under the protection of the state. Naturally there corresponds to the positive conception of the state a negative conception of the non-state in two principal and reinforcing visions: the wild state from Lucretius to Vico, which goes from the savage state of primitive peoples to a version of the state of anarchy, understood by Hobbes as the war of all against all. The two versions differ in this: for the first, the non-state is a superable phase of human history and, in fact, in many nations it has been overcome, whereas the second state is one into which humankind can always fall back (as happens when a civil war occurs).

Discussions about the best republic are linked to the positive conception of the state, which presupposes that existing states are imperfect but perfectable, and therefore the state as an organized attempt at civilized cohabitation is not to be destroyed but to be brought to a full realization of its proper essence. The extreme form of the outlining

of the optimum republic can be found in the sketches of
ideal republics, of republics that have never existed and
will never be realized in any place (or are located in
imaginary places) and are proposed as limiting ideals of a
perfectly rational arrangement whereby every sort of
behaviour is rigorously foreseen and rigidly regulated. From
Plato's *Republic* to Tommaso Campanella's *Citta del Sole*,
ideal republics have always been models of hyper-statization,
of a genuine overgrowth of the function of the regulation
of civil life from which the need for political life would
originate, and consequently they are representations
inspired by a highly positive conception of the state (whose
counterfigure is the negative Utopia of Orwell, which is a
response to the real or foreseeable abuses of the total
state).

The state as a necessary evil

There are two negative conceptions of the state, one weak
and one strong: the state as a necessary evil and the state
as an unnecessary evil. Only the second leads to the idea
of the end of the state.

The negative conception of the state as a necessary evil
has presented itself in the history of political theory in two
different forms depending on whether the state is judged
from the point of view of the church-non-state or the civil
society-non-state.

In the first form characteristic of early Christian thought
the state was necessary as a *remedium peccati* because the
masses are wicked and must be held back by fear (that fear
which, for Montesquieu, will be the principle of despotism
and, for Robespierre, connected to virtue, the principle of
revolutionary government): *In gentibus principes regesque
electi sunt ut terrore suo populos a malo coercerent atque
ad recte vivendum legibus subderent* (Isidore of Seville,
Sententiae, III, 477, in Migne, *Patriologia latina*, LXXXIII,
col. 717). Abandoned by scholastic thought which, under
the influence of the classical doctrine, rediscovered the

thesis of the positive function of civil government, the negative doctrine of the state was taken up again by Luther with a vehemence equalled only by the doctrine that will justify state terrorism in the celebrated letter to Christian princes, *On secular authority* (1523), where one reads that true Christians being few,

God has imposed on others besides . . . the rule of God, another regime and he has placed them under the sword so that even if they wanted to they could not exercise their wickedness and when they do it is not without fear or with peace and happiness; like one ties a savage and fierce beast with shackles and chains so that it cannot bite or attack in accordance with its instinct, even if it could do so voluntarily.

Beyond every religious vision the negative conception of the state appears in the stream of realistic political thought grounded on a pessimistic anthropology; from some famous sayings of Machiavelli, the image of the 'devilish face' of power has derived. But the connection between a pessimistic anthropology and a negative conception of the state is not necessary. Hobbes has a pessimistic vision of individuals who, left to their own devices, are as wolves to other people; however, Leviathan is the beneficial monster opposed to Behemoth, the evil monster of civil war.

While admitting that the state is a necessary evil, none of these doctrines does away with the ideal of the end of the state. In the Christian vision of the world beyond (even above) the state there is a church which makes use of the state for good and therefore needs it even if it considers it an imperfect instrument. The negativity of the state is not without redemption in its subordination to the church (while in the realistic conception of the state there is no redemption except in the power that is the ultimate aim of the prince). For this reason, even in its negativity the state must survive: *Et licet peccatum humanae originis per baptismi gratiam cunctis fidelibus dimissum sit, tamen aequus deus ideo discrevit hominibus vitam, alios servos constituens, alios dominos, ut licentia male agendi a servorum potestate dominantium restringatur* (Isidore of Seville, *Sententiae*, III, 47, i, in Migne, *Patrologia latina*, LXXXIII, col.717).

When civil society in the form of free market society advances the claim to restrict the powers of the state to the minimum necessary, the state as a necessary evil becomes the minimal state, an image that becomes common in liberal theory. For Adam Smith the state must confine itself to providing external defence and internal order as well as the execution of public works. Nobody has expressed the idea of the minimal state more incisively than Thomas Paine. Right at the beginning of *Common Sense* he writes:

Society is produced by our wants and government by our wickedness; the former promotes our happiness *positively* by uniting our affections, the latter *negatively* by restraining our vices. The one encourages intercourse, the other creates distinctions. The first is a patron, the last a punisher. Society in every state is a blessing, but government even in its best state is but a necessary evil, in its worst state an intolerable one. (1776)

From William von Humboldt to Benjamin Constant, from J.S. Mill to Herbert Spencer, the theory that the best state is the one that governs least dominates as bourgeois society expands and – to tell the truth more in theory than practice – as the idea of the free internal and international markets (freedom of exchange) triumphs. But even in this case the minimal state does not mean society without the state. The theory of the minimal state does not coincide with any of the forms that anarchism assumed in the same century. A book that has recently had such great success as to be compared to J.S. Mill's *On Liberty* (1859) is Robert Nozick's *Anarchy, State and Utopia* (1974), which sets itself the task of defending the minimalist state both against the anarchist negation of the state and against the state of justice, especially against John Rawls' (1971) much-discussed thesis, arguing subtly and at length in favour of the thesis that 'the minimalist State is the most extended State it is possible to justify' (Nozick 1974).

A variation on the theory of the minimalist state,

bordering on the theory of the end of the state, is the Anglo-Saxon doctrine of guild socialism which elaborates a genuine theory of the pluralistic society founded on the distinction between functional decentralization of groups and territorial decentralization, and on the thesis that the state should restrict its role to that of the supreme coordinator of functional, economic and cultural groups. Georges Gurvitch's *La déclaration des droits sociaux* (1944) can be considered the manifesto of social and legal pluralism which has its distant origins in Proudhon: the individual must be taken into account not as an abstract entity but as a producer, consumer, citizen; to each activity must correspond some associational function and the state, as a supra-functional entity, has the job of coordination and not domination.

The state as an unnecessary evil

And what if the state were an evil and not even a necessary one? A positive answer to this question has inspired various theories of the end of the state. It should be mentioned that in all these theories the state is understood as the holder of the monopoly of force and the only power on a given territory that has the means to restrain reprobates and recalcitrants even to the point of using coercion in the last instance. The end of the state, therefore, means the birth of a society that can survive and prosper without a coercive apparatus. Beyond the minimalist state which has liberated itself, first from the monopolization of ideological power, allowing the expression of the most diverse religious beliefs and political opinions, then from the monopolization of economic power, allowing the free possession and transmission of goods, there is the final emancipation of the non-state from the state, society without the state which has also been liberated from the need for coercive power. The ideal of a society without the state is a universalistic ideal: the 'republic of wise men' aspired to by the Stoics who, however, thought the state necessary for the masses, or the monastery life which does not spurn, when necessary, the protection of the powerful of this world, can both be interpreted as prefigurations of a society without a state, but these alone do not prove its realizability.

The most popular of the theories that supports the realizability and even the necessary advent of a society without a state is Marx's, or rather Engels's on the reasoning which, reduced to its barest, can be laid out like this: the state develops from the division of society into classes opposed (because of the division of labour), with the intention of allowing the class on top to dominate the class below; when, following the conquest of power by the universal class (the dictatorship of the proletariat), class-divided society will disappear, so will the necessity of the state. This is perhaps the most ingenious theory amongst those that defend the ideal of society without the state but it is no less debatable for that. Neither the major premiss of the syllogism (the state is an instrument of class domination) nor the minor premiss (the universal class is destined to destroy class society) have resisted that formidable argument which is, as Hegel would have said, 'the harsh reply of history'.

The Marx–Engels theory of the end of the state is certainly one of the most popular but it is not the only one. At least three others can be pointed to without making any claim at being comprehensive. Above all there is the ancient and continually recurring religious aspiration to a society without a state common to many heretical Christian sects which, preaching a return to evangelical sources, to a religion of non-violence and universal brotherhood, refuse obedience to the laws of the state, do not recognize its two essential institutions (the army and the courts), and declare that a community living in conformity with evangelical precepts will not need political institutions. At the opposite extreme the ideal of the end of political society, and of the political class that draws an unfair advantage from it, was preached by a conception of the state that today would be called technocratic, like that proposed by St Simon according to which in industrial society the protagonists are no longer the warriors and lawyers but the scientists and producers, and there will no longer be need of 'Caesar's sword'. This technocratic ideal, in St Simon, is accompanied by a strong religious fervour (the *nouveau Christianisme*), almost suggesting the idea that the leap out of history that is a society without a state is not conceivable outside the messianic idea. At the same time, the technocratic model has exercised a strong influence on some Marxist theorists. Just think of what has been called Bucharin's '*rêve mathématique*', expressed so clearly in some propositions of the *ABC of Communism*, according to which, once the revolution has come, 'the central direction [in communist society] will be entrusted to various accounting and statistical offices' (Bukharin and Preobraženskij 1919).

Finally, the idea of a society without a state has given rise to a genuine current of political thought and to various corresponding movements which, since the end of the eighteenth century, have not ceased to fuel political debate or invite deeds appropriate for the ideal fought for: anarchism. Taking to extremes the ideal of the liberation of humankind from every form of authority – religious, political and economic – and seeing the state as the greatest form of oppression of person over person, anarchism aspires to a society without state or laws founded on a spontaneous and voluntary cooperation of associated individuals, free and equal amongst themselves. Despite all its variations – whether because of philosophical presuppositions or choice of means (persuasion or violence) or all the different political and economic reforms it promotes – anarchism represents an ever-recurring ideal of a society without oppressors or oppressed. It is founded more on an optimistic notion of humankind rather than religious conviction or theoretical scientific claims, diametrically opposed to that conception which invokes the state to calm the 'savage beast'.

4

Democracy and Dictatorship

Since the classical age, the term 'democracy' has always been used to designate one of the forms of government, or rather one of the various ways in which political power can be exercised. Specifically, it designates that form of government in which political power is exercised by the people. In the history of political theory, a discussion of the characteristics, the merits and the defects of democracy is to be found in the theory and typology of governmental forms. Consequently, no account of democracy can avoid stating the relationship between democracy and other forms of government, because only in this way can its specific character be described. In other words, as the concept of democracy belongs to a system of concepts constituting the theory of governmental forms, it can only be understood in relation to the other concepts of the system which it helps to define and is in turn defined by. A division of approaches to the concept of democracy can be made by placing it in the larger conceptual network of the theory of governmental forms and noting the various uses to which this has been put at different times and by different authors. The following three uses exist: the descriptive (or systematic), the evaluative (or axiological) and the historical. In its descriptive or systematic use, a theory of governmental forms consists of the classification and typology of histori-cally existing forms of government carried out on the basis of shared and distinguished characteristics, similar to the operation in botany which classifies plants and in zoology which classifies animals. In its evaluative or axiological use, a theory of governmental forms consists of a series of value judgements in which different constitutions are not merely compared to each other, but ranked as one is judged good and the other bad, one excellent and the other terrible, one better than, or not so bad, as the other, and so on. Finally, it is possible to speak of a historical use of the theory of governmental forms when it serves not just to classify different constitutions, and not only to recommend one over another, but also to describe the different stages of historical development as a series of necessary transitions from one form to another. When, as often happens, the evaluative and historical uses are joined together, the description of the different historical stages becomes a theory of progress or decline, depending on whether the best form is at the beginning or end of the cycle.

Starting from this premise the first part of this chapter is devoted to illustrating the various ways in which democracy has been treated in the most important historical typologies (see the following section), and taking account of the opposed evaluations it has been subjected to in different times and by different authors (in the third section). Finally, it gives an indication of the place democracy has been assigned in some of the main philosophies of history that have used the transition from one form of government to another to mark stages of historical development (discussed in the fourth section). It is hardly necessary to warn that the three uses are rarely completely separate and that the same typology often contains a mixture of all three. A classical example is the celebrated theory of governmental forms contained in the eighth book of Plato's *Republic*, which describes the specific characteristics of different constitutions and, at the same time, ranks them from best to worst: a hierarchical ordering that corresponds to their chronological ordering from ancient to more recent times.

After this first part, in which democracy appears as an

element in a conceptual network, the second part will be devoted to the analysis of democracy in its various interpretations and historical manifestations: in particular, to the distinctions between ancient and modern democracy, representative and direct democracy, political and social democracy and formal and substantive democracy.

In the third part, different interpretations of dictatorship will be compared to these various forms of democracy: specifically, the dictatorship of the ancients, which is contrasted with modern dictatorship and, especially, revolutionary dictatorship.

THE DESCRIPTIVE USE

In its descriptive meaning, according to the classical tradition, democracy is one of three possible governmental forms in the typology which classifies such forms depending on the different numbers of rulers; more precisely, it is that form of government in which power is exercised by all the people, or by the greater part, or by the masses. As such it is distinguished from monarchy and from aristocracy in which power is exercised either by one or by few. In Plato's *The Statesman* the celebrated tripartite division is introduced in the following manner:

Monarchy is one of the forms of political power, is it not? Yes.
And after monarchy we can, I believe, locate the rule of the few. Why not?
And is not the third form of government the power of the multitude and is it not called by the name of democracy? (291d)

Distinctions between forms of government according to the number of rulers are taken up again by Aristotle with these words: 'It is necesssary that sovereign power be exercised by one alone, by the few or by the many' (*Politics*, 1279a). Aristotle places classification on the basis of number alongside the one based on the various ways of governing (for the common good or for the good of those who govern), from which he derives the no less famous distinction between good and bad forms. He reserves the term 'democracy' for the bad form, while the good form is given the more general name which means constitution, *politeia*. In the third fundamental text of the classical tradition, a passage from the sixth book of Polybius' *Histories*, the theory of governmental forms is introduced thus: 'The majority of those who have dealt with these arguments teach us that there exist three forms of government called respectively kingship, aristocracy and democracy' (VI, 3). The term 'democracy' reverts to describing the government by the many in its positive aspect: 'ochlocracy' is the term assigned by Polybius to its bad form. It remains clear that in a classical typology, which uses the number of rulers to distinguish between various constitutions, there is a form of government, which may or may not be called democracy, which differs from the others in being the government by the many rather than the few, or by the more rather than the less, or by the majority rather than the minority or a restricted group of persons (even one alone).

As handed down to us, therefore, the ancient concept of democracy is both extremely simple and constant. To cite just some of the classics of political philosophy, this meaning of democracy, involving the tripartite division of the forms of government and based on number, is found in Marsilius of Padua's *Defensor Pacis*, in Machiavelli's *Discourses,* in Bodin's *De la république*, in the political works of Hobbes, in Spinoza, Locke, Vico and, with particular emphasis not on the possession but on the exercise of sovereign power, in Rousseau's *Contrat Social*.

Despite its prevalence the threefold division is sometimes replaced by a twofold one. Two different manoeuvres can effect this rearrangement: either by regrouping democracy and aristocracy together and opposing them to monarchy, or by regrouping monarchy and aristocracy and opposing them to democracy. Machiavelli brought about the first realignment in the opening lines of *The Prince*, where it can be read that 'all states and dominions which hold or have held sway over mankind are either republics or monarchies' (1513). The second realignment has prevailed in modern political theory where the classical tripartite division has been universally replaced by the primary and fundamental distinction between democracy and autocracy. One of the authors who contributed to the diffusion and consolidation of this distinction was Kelsen. In his *General Theory of the Law and State* (1945), after noting the superficiality of the traditional division based on number, he adopts the distinctive criterion of greater or less political liberty, and concludes that 'it is now more precise to distinguish between two types of constitution, instead of three: democracy and autocracy.'

The Machiavellian distinction (taken up again by Montesquieu who, however, returned to the tripartite division, adding despotism as a third form to monarchy and the republic) is still based on the criterion of number, even if it is dominated by the idea that the essential distinction is between the government of one (which can only be a physical person) and the government by an assembly (which can only be a legal person, whether it is an assembly of aristocrats or of representatives of the people). Consequently, democracy and aristocracy are best considered as just one species under the general name of republic (which can, in fact, be either democratic or aristocratic).

The distinction between democracy and autocracy is founded on a completely different criterion: namely, that power either ascends from bottom to top or descends from top to bottom. To justify this, Kelsen makes use of the distinction between autonomy and heteronomy: democratic forms of government are those in which the laws are made by the same people to whom they apply (and for that reason they are autonomous norms), while in autocratic forms of government the law-makers are different from those to whom the laws are addressed (and are therefore heteronomous norms). So while the classification found at the birth of the modern state has absorbed democracy into a more general concept of republic, the more widespread classification of modern political theory absorbs monarchy and aristocracy together in the more general concept of autocracy, and gives particular prominence to democracy seen as one of the two poles on which all existing constitutions, to a greater or lesser extent, converge.

THE EVALUATIVE USE

Like any other form of government democracy can be evaluated, either as a good form to be praised or recommended or as a bad form to be blamed and condemned. The entire history of political thought is riddled with disputes about the best form of government and within this dispute a recurrent theme has been the argument for and against democracy.

The start of this dispute can be seen in the discussion referred to by Herodotus (*The Histories*, III, sections 80–2) between three Persians, Otanes, Megabyzus and Darius, on the best form of government to install in Persia after the death of Cambyses. Each of them defends one of the three classical forms and attempts to refute the other two. Otanes, the defender of democracy, after criticizing monarchical government because the monarch 'can do just as he wants without being responsible to anyone', gives government by the people 'the name more lovely than any other: equality of rights', and defines it as that in which 'the government is accountable and all decisions are taken in common.' The defender of aristocracy, Megabyzus, and the defender of monarchy, Darius, both offer arguments to show that government by the people is a bad form. The first finds nothing more silly or insolent than a 'good-for-nothing mob' and concludes that it is not permissible 'to flee the overbearingness of the tyrant by bowing to the insolence of an unleashed mob'. For the second, 'when the people govern it is impossible to prevent corruption in the public domain, which does not generate hostility but, on the contrary, solid friendships between ne'er-do-wells.'

In this dispute, which would have taken place in the.

second half of the sixth century BC and which was reported in a text of the following century, some of the arguments against democracy were presented and fixed once and for all. In Greek thought praise and blame come close to one another. Pericles offered the most famous praise in his speech to the Athenians in honour of the first dead of the Peloponnesian war.

We live under a form of government which does not emulate the institutions of our neighbours; on the contrary, we are ourselves a model which some follow, rather than the imitators of other peoples. It is true that our government is called a democracy, because its administration is in the hands, not of the few, but of the many; yet while as regards the law all men are on an equality for the settlement of their private disputes, as regards the value set on them it is as each man is in any way distinguished that he is preferred to public honours, not because he belongs to a particular class, but because of personal merits; nor, again, on the ground of poverty is a man barred from a public career by obscurity of rank if he but has it in him to do the state a service. And not only in our public life are we liberal, but also as regards our freedom from suspicion of one another in the pursuits of every-day life; for we do not feel resentment at our neighbour if he does as he likes, nor yet do we put on sour looks which, though harmless, are painful to behold. But while we thus avoid giving offence in our private intercourse, in our public life we are restrained from lawlessness chiefly through reverent fear, for we render obedience to those in authority and to the laws, and especially to those laws which are ordained for the succour of the oppressed and those which, though unwritten, bring upon the transgressor a disgrace which all men recognize. (Thucydides, *History of the Peloponnesian War*, II, 37)

In this passage democracy is considered a good form of government on account of the following features: it is a government in favour of the many and not the few; the law is equal for rich and poor alike and therefore it is a government of laws, whether written or not, and not of individuals; and liberty is respected both in private and in public life, where what counts is not adherence to any particular party but merit.

However, the most celebrated condemnation is found in the eighth book of Plato's *Republic,* where democracy is described as a degenerate form, though not the most degenerate, which is tyranny. The four degenerate forms are matched against the ideal of the city state and ranked in order of increasing degeneration: timocracy, oligarchy, democracy and tyranny. While oligarchy is the government of the rich, democracy is the government not of the people but of the poor against the rich. The principle of democracy is liberty, but it is a liberty which is abruptly transformed into licence due to the lack of moral and political restraint characteristic of democratic people, due to the upsurge of immodest desire and superfluous needs, because of lack of respect for the law and a general tendency to subvert authority so that parents fear their children, 'the master fears and flatters his pupils and the pupils laugh at their masters and teachers' (563a).

The distinction between the three good constitutions and the three bad constitutions which is based on the criterion of whether government is in the common interest or is self-interested, and which was to become one of the commonplaces of later political thought, receives its first definitive statement in Aristotle. In this typology government by the masses appears in its good form under the name of *politeia* and in its bad form under the name of democracy. Like Plato, Aristotle defines democracy as the government by the poor and consequently by the many, but only because in most states the poor are more numerous than the rich. But the government of the poor is just as self-interested as government of the rich and it is equally corrupt given that the criterion of good government is attention to the common interest. In Polybius, the names change but the arrangement into three good and three bad forms of government remains. The good form of popular government is democracy in which the people 'take on themselves the care of the public interest'; the bad form, ochlocracy (or government by the plebs), is the degeneration of democracy:

For the people, having grown accustomed to feed at the expense of others and to depend for their livelihood on the property of others, as soon as they find a leader who is enterprising but is excluded from the honours of office by his penury, institute the rule of violence; and now uniting their forces massacre, banish, and plunder, until they degenerate again into perfect savages and find once more a master and monarch. (Polybius, *Histories*, VI, 9)

When used prescriptively, the typology of governmental forms contains both absolute and relative judgements. From this point of view the dispute about democracy is not just concerned with whether democracy is a good or bad form but whether it is better or worse than the others. There are three possibilities in a typology that does not distinguish pure from corrupt forms: that democracy might be the worst, the best or somewhere in between. Historically, the most frequent and important theses are the first two since the comparison is usually made between the two extreme forms which are, in fact, monarchy and democracy. In a typology which does distinguish between pure and corrupt forms of constitutions, the comparison becomes more complex: democracy can be either the worst (or the best) of the good forms or the best (or the worst) of the bad forms. In Greek thought the two most frequent theses derive from Plato (from *The Statesman*) and Polybius.

For Plato, democracy is at the same time the worst of the good forms and the best of the bad forms (whereas monarchy is the best of the good forms and the worst of the bad forms), with the consequence that the difference between good and bad democracy is minimal (whereas there is a great difference between monarchy and tyranny). Polybius, on the other hand, ranks democracy at the bottom of both the good and bad scales; that is to say, it is the worst of both the good and bad forms. In the typology of Plato's *Republic*, which only deals with degenerate forms, the evaluative problem is to assign a place to democracy in the process of continuing degeneration; for Plato it is worse than timocracy and oligarchy but better than tyranny.

Finally, in a typology such as Vico's which only recognizes good forms – good in the sense that every form corresponds to a definite stage in the development of humanity (to the *Zeitgeist*, as Hegel will eventually put it) – the evaluative problem is to assign democracy its proper place in the process of ongoing perfection. For Vico democracy or, to use Vico's terminology, the popular republic, is better than the aristocratic republic but worse than a principality. (For Vico as well as Plato, government by the people is not an extreme form – that is, a form found at the beginning or end of a series as in most political theories – but an intermediate form.)

In the dispute about the best forms of government the classics of modern political thought (whose insights accompanied the rise and consolidation of largely monarchical, territorial states) have been, at least up until the French Revolution (and with the exception of Spinoza), in favour of monarchy and against democracy. Among these are Bodin, Hobbes, Locke, Vico, Montesquieu, Kant and Hegel. While some of these authors (Vico, for example), looking at the various forms of government in their historical development, exalt monarchy as the form of government most adapted to their age, others (such as Hobbes and Bodin) make an abstract comparison of all the traditional arguments against government by the people and of all the ancient and modern grounds against democracy (and which later turn up in the right-wing propaganda of our day without any noticeable changes). The tenth chapter of Hobbes's *De cive*, entitled *Specierum trium civitatis quoad incommoda singularum comparatio*, can be considered paradigmatic: the arguments against democracy may be divided into two groups: those which deal with the governing subject (the popular assembly compared to the undivided power of the monarch) and those which deal with the manner of governing. The defects of a popular assembly are incompetence, the dominance of eloquence (and, therefore, of demagogy), the development of parties which block the formation of a collective will and favour rapid changes in the law and, finally, the lack of secrecy. The disadvantages of power exercised by the people consist in greater corruption (because in a democracy there are many starving people who have to be made happy by their leaders), and less security because of the protection that the demagogues are forced to extend to their supporters; moreover, this increased corruption and insecurity is not compensated for by greater liberty.

Spinoza's *Tractatus* was written to demonstrate the superiority of democratic government but, unfortunately, the section dedicated to this form of government was left incomplete. However, when comparing Hobbes and Spinoza (legitimately comparable because of the similarity of their first principles), it is possible to understand why Spinoza, although starting from the same realistic vision of power and the same way of conceptualizing the state, arrived at a radically different conclusion from Hobbes in comparing the different forms of government. What divides them is the ultimate goal of the state which is peace and order for Hobbes and liberty for Spinoza. This difference rests, in turn, on another, even deeper, difference that allows us above all to contrast one theory with the other: namely the difference based on the dominant perspective chosen by every political writer and which makes it possible to contrast writers who look at things *ex parte principis* (that is, from the ruler's point of view in order to justify their right of command and the subjects' duty to obey) with writers who see things *ex parte populi* (or, in other words, from the point of view of the ruled in order to justify their right not to be oppressed and the ruler's duty to proclaim just laws). There are those who hold that the main problem of the state is to maintain the unity of power, even to the extent of damaging the liberty of individuals; and there are those who propose that the main problem of the state is to maintain individual liberty even to the extent of endangering its own unity.

The argument between the proponents of monarchy and the proponents of democracy is an argument between two parties which analyse and evaluate the same problem from completely different points of view. The solution offered by those who advocate democracy (which is the problem of the state seen from the point of view of the ruled), is ultimately the identification of the rulers with the ruled or, rather, the elimination of the ruler as a figure separate from the ruled. This identification is clearly set out in Spinoza who, expounding the 'foundations of democratic government', affirms that 'in it . . . no one transfers their own natural rights to another in so definitive a manner that they can no longer be consulted; instead, they delegate it to the greater part of the whole society of which they are a member. Thus everyone continues to be as equal as they were in the preceding state of nature' (1670). This statement cannot fail to bring to mind the central idea which inspired the work of the man considered to be the father of modern democracy: the idea of a society through which 'each one, by uniting with all, obeys no one but himself, remaining free as before' (Rousseau, 1762).

The Rousseauistic theme of liberty as autonomy, on the definition of liberty as 'the obedience of everyone to the law he has prescribed himself' became, after the American and the French Revolutions and after the birth of the first socialist and anarchist ideas, if not *the* main, then one of the main arguments in favour of democracy in the face of every other sort of government (which if not democratic must be autocratic). The problem of democracy became more and more identified with the theme of self-government and the progress of democracy with the expansion of those areas in which the method of self-government was being put to the proof. From the beginning of the last century until today the development of democracy coincided with the progressive expansion of political rights: that is, the right to participate, if only through the election of representatives, in the formation of the collective will. The progress of democracy goes hand-in-hand with the conviction that, after the age of Enlightenment, humankind (to paraphrase Kant) left the age of minority and as an adult, and no longer a pupil, must freely decide about both individual lives and collective life. As an ever-increasing number of individuals acquire the right to participate in political life, autocracy regresses and democracy advances. Alongside the ethical argument in favour of democracy, which is seen as the political manifestation of the supreme value of liberty, the positive evaluation of democracy–autonomy compared to autocracy–heteronomy deploys two other arguments, one of which is more properly political and the other more generally utilitarian. The political argument is founded on one of the most agreed-upon maxims in all political thought: the maxim that power tends to corrupt. The history of political thought can be seen as a long, uninterrupted and impassioned discussion about the various ways of limiting the exercise of power and, of course, democracy is one of these. One of the strongest arguments in favour of democracy is that the people cannot use power against their own interests or, to put it another way, when the legislator and the addressee of a law are one and the same, the first cannot abuse the second. The utilitarian argument is founded on another maxim of experience (not so well-founded, to be sure), which claims that the best interpreters of the collective interest are those who belong to the collectivity whose interest is at stake – that is, they have the same interests – and in this sense, *vox populi vox dei*.

THE HISTORICAL USE

For centuries, at least until Hegel, the major political writers used the typology of governmental forms to outline the development of human history understood as the succession of one type of constitution by another according to a certain rhythm. The question here is, what place did democracy occupy in some of the more important systems? It is necessary, first of all, to distinguish between regressive philosophies of history, in which successive stages are increasingly degenerate; and progressive philosophies in which successive stages are an improvement on the preceding one; and cyclical philosophies, in which there is a return to the beginning after having run through all the progressive or regressive stages. In regressive histories (Plato) or cyclical–regressive histories (Polybius) democracy generally occupies the third place in a series which puts monarchy first, aristocracy second and democracy third. The best example of this is Polybius (and not just for this but also in view of his influence on modern writers; Machiavelli in the second chapter of the *Discourses* springs to mind) whose periodization presents in rapid synthesis a series of the six forms alternating between the good forms and their respective bad forms:

Spontaneously and naturally, monarchy arises first and through a series of opportune corrections and transformations kingship is derived from it. When this falls prey to the natural defects which transform it into tyranny, it is abolished and replaced by aristocracy. When, by natural process, this degenerates into oligarchy and the people indignantly punish the injustices of their chiefs, democracy springs up. When it in its turn is tarnished by illegality and violence it turns into ochlocracy. (*Histories*, VI, 4)

In the modern age of the great monarchies, when the regressive conception yielded to the progressive, the writer's observational range was greatly extended and the cycle of the ancients was reversed: monarchy was no longer at the beginning of the cycle but the end. Vico was considered an innovator because after the savage condition (not yet social) and state of the family (which was not yet a state) he began the history of states not with monarchy but with an aristocratic republic, followed by the popular republic and finally the principality. In *De universi iuris uno principio et uno fine,* popular government is defined as that where 'equal suffrage, free speech and the equal access of all to honours, including the highest, notwithstanding birth or inheritance' (1720) are in force (the principle that the basis of political rights is wealth lasts, as already noted, until the

French revolution and beyond). One characteristic of the Vichian typology, however, is that it is transformed into a dichotomy in a different manner from those already pointed out: the two most noted dichotomies are monarchy and republic (with democracy and aristocracy reduced to one) and democracy and autocracy (with monarchy and aristocracy reduced to one). For Vico, the essential difference is between, on the one hand, the aristocratic republic representing the heroic age, and on the other popular republic and monarchy which both represent the merely human age. The classical trichotomy, therefore, may be turned into the dichotomy between aristocracy and 'human governments' (that is, democracy and monarchy) in which:

in virtue of the equality of the intelligent nature which is the proper nature of man, all are accounted equal under the laws, inasmuch as all are born free in their cities. This is the case in the free popular cities in which all or the majority make up the just forces of the city, in virtue of which they are the lords of popular liberty. It is also the case in monarchies, in which the monarchs make all their subjects equal under their laws, and, having all the force of arms in their own hands, are themselves the only bearers of any distinction in civil nature. (1744, section 927)

In Montesquieu's important classification of governmental forms, expounded and illustrated in detail in the *Esprit des lois*, monarchy appears again as the form of government most adapted to the large European territorial states. Despotism is the form most adapted to oriental peoples, and the republic (which, following Machiavelli, can be either democratic or aristocratic) the most suitable for the ancient world. By its nature, republican government is defined as that in which 'the people as a body, or certain families, enjoy supreme power' (1748): according to the principle, or the 'spring' which motivates it, it is characterized by virtue (while monarchy has honour as its governing principle, and despotism, fear). In both chapters devoted to the nature of democracy and to its governing principle, examples are taken from Greek and Roman history and one finds the following statement: 'Greek politicians, who lived under a popular government, recognised in virtue the only force capable of sustaining them. Today's politicians speak only of manufacture, commerce, finance, riches and luxury' (Montesquieu 1748), and the origin of the definition of virtue as 'love of the republic' is obviously classical. The nature and governing principle of despotism are illustrated with examples dealing with oriental peoples; the nature and principle of monarchy with examples dealing with the great European states of Spain, France and England.

Montesquieu's tripartite division becomes a fundamental principle for the interpretation of the course of human history in Hegel's philosophy, the last great philosophy of history to chart the evolution of civilization through the change from one form of government to another (after Hegel, most philosophies of history took the evolution of social forms, the relations of production and so on as their markers). The principal elements which will shape the general design of the immense material of his mature philosophy of history can already be seen in a juvenile work: 'The continuity of world culture, after oriental despotism and the degeneration of that republic which dominated the world, has brought humanity to an intermediate position' which is 'the system of representation' found 'in all modern European States' (1799–1802). In the *Lectures on the Philosophy of History*, the theme is taken up again and its main elements expounded as follows:

Universal history is a process of the education of man away from the unrestrained character of natural will towards universal and subjective liberty. The Orient knew and only knows that one alone is free, the Greek and Roman worlds that some are free, the Germanic world that all are free. The first form, then, which we see in universal history is *despotism*, the second is *democracy* and *aristocracy*, and the third is *monarchy*. (1830–1)

For Hegel, then, as for most writers who reflect on the formation and growth of the modern state, democracy is a form of government which belongs to the past. In the work that represents the essence of his political thought, *The Philosophy of Right*, Hegel writes against the concept of popular sovereignty which is the antithesis of monarchical sovereignty: 'Taken without its monarch and the articulation of the whole which is the indispensable and direct concomitant of monarchy, the people is a formless mass and no longer a State. It lacks every one of those determinate characteristics – sovereignty, government, judges, magistrates, class-divisions, etc., – which are to be found only in a whole which is inwardly organized' (1821, section 279 annotation). By making constitutional monarchy the culminating moment of historical development Hegel, the philosopher of the age of restoration, brought an epoch to a close.

MODERN DEMOCRACY

At the time of the formation of the great territorial states, which were brought into being by the centralizing and unifying activities of princes, the now classical argument against democracy consisted in pointing out that democratic government was only possible in small states. Even Rousseau was convinced that a real democracy had never existed because it required, among other conditions, the existence of a small state 'in which the people would find it easy to meet and in which every citizen could easily get to know all the others' (1762). But just as Hegel was praising constitutional monarchy as the only form of government after the French Revolution in which world spirit might recognize itself, a republican government was born in an enormous territory, destined to become larger than that occupied by the principal European states and sufficiently strong to attract the attention and admiration of some restless and clear-sighted spirits: the United States of America.

To tell the truth, some of the founding fathers of the new state, who were to demonstrate in their theoretical debates and in constitutional construction that they were well acquainted with both classical and modern political thought, did not want the republic they were aiming at and to which they had committed their energies to be confused with the democracy of the ancients. James Madison's judgement on ancient democracy (*The Federalist*, no. 10) can hardly be distinguished from that of the most relentless of anti-democrats: 'Hence it is that such democracies have ever been spectacles of turbulence and contention; have ever been found incompatible with personal security or the rights of property; and have in general been as short in their lives as they have been violent in their deaths.' But Madison, following the tradition of the classics handed on to Rousseau, was referring to direct democracy. By 'republic' he meant representative democracy, exactly that form of government which today we, convinced that only representative democracy is viable in large states, call democracy (without any further specification) and which we oppose to all old and new forms of autocracy. Madison wrote: 'The two great points of difference between a democracy and a republic are: first, the delegation of the government, in the latter, to a small number of citizens elected by the rest; secondly, the greater number of citizens, and greater sphere of country, over which the latter may be extended' (*The Federalist*, no. 10). The definite view emerging from this passsage is that there exists a necessary link between the representative state (or republic) and territorial dimension, and that the only non-autocratic form of government possible in a large territory and with a large population (even if that of the United States was very sparse) is government by representation, a democratic form of government which is corrected, limited and temperate. The following quotation confirms that the changeover from direct to indirect democracy is objectively determined by external factors and that therefore the republic is not so much opposed to democracy as the only sort of democracy possible in given types of territory and population: 'The other point of difference is, the greater number of citizens and extent of territory which may be brought within the compass of republican than of democratic government; and it is this circumstance principally which renders factious combinations less to be dreaded in the former than in the latter.'

It is to Alexis de Tocqueville, in the first volume of *Democracy in America*, published in 1835, that the recognition, the consecration almost, is owed of the new state of the New World as a genuine form of modern democracy in contrast to ancient democracy. In the preface to the 1848 edition, de Tocqueville wrote that America had all but solved the problem of democratic liberty which Europe was only just then confronting: 'The principle of popular sovereignty which we have only just introduced into our country has reigned supreme in America for sixty years and there it has been put into practice in the most direct, most unlimited, most absolute way' (1848). For the writer of these words, the distinction between direct and representative democracy no longer has any relevance: 'Sometimes the people itself makes the laws, as in Athens; at other times deputies, elected by a universal suffrage represent it and act in its name under almost direct surveillance.' What matters is that power is really in the hands of the people, whether directly or through representatives who enforce the 'law of laws' (that is, the principle of popular sovereignty) so that 'society acts of its own accord' and 'power does not exist outside it and there is no one who would dare to believe, let alone express, the idea of looking for power elsewhere.' The chapter on the principle of popular sovereignty concludes with these words: 'The people reign over the American political world like God over the universe. It is the beginning and end of everything: everything springs from it and everything leads back to it' (de Tocqueville, 1835–40).

In contrast to the democracy of the ancients which is founded on government by assembly and which recognizes no intermediary between the state and the individual, and in whose name Rousseau, its modern advocate, condemns particular associations as guilty of dividing what should remain united, modern democracy is pluralistic and lives on the existence, the multiplicity and the vigour of intermediate associations. De Tocqueville was struck both by the equality of conditions and by the tendency of members of American society to join associations in order to promote the public good, so that 'independently of the permanent associations created by law in the name of the community, the city and the country, there also existed a host of others which owed their existence and development to the will of individuals' (1835–40). And associationism became a new criterion (new compared to the traditional criteria which focused exclusively on the number of rulers) for distinguishing between democratic and non-democratic societies as is shown by this surprisingly incisive passage:

In aristocratic society men have no need to unite in order to act because they are already firmly held together. Every rich and powerful citizen is like the head of a permanent and strong association which includes everybody dependent on him and whom he bids carry out his plans. In democracies where all citizens are independent and inefficient, they can do hardly anything alone and no one is able to oblige his peers to cooperate. If they do not learn to help each other freely, they all fall into helplessness. (de Tocqueville 1835–40)

REPRESENTATIVE DEMOCRACY AND DIRECT DEMOCRACY

In the century before the First World War, the history of democracy coincides with the consolidation of the representative state in the main European countries and with their internal development: so much so that the complex typology of traditional forms of government is reduced to the opposition of the types, democracy and autocracy. Bearing in mind the two fundamental characteristics of American democracy highlighted by de Tocqueville (the principle of popular sovereignty and the phenomenon of associations), the representative state which was gradually being consolidated in England and, from there, diffused throughout most other European states by the early nineteenth century, the constitutional movement consisted in a process of democratization along two lines: the enlargement of the right to vote up to the point of universal suffrage for both men and women, and the development of political associations until mass political parties were formed and their public functions recognized.

Nothing illustrates this two-pronged process better than a comparison of the Statute of the King of Sardinia, promulgated by Carlo Alberto on 4 March 1848, and which was later to become the first written constitution of the Kingdom of Italy (1861), with the Republican Constitution elaborated and approved by the Constituent Assembly, elected on 2 June 1946 and which entered into force almost exactly a century after the Albertine Statute, on 1 January 1948. First of all, through successive extensions of political rights in 1882, 1912, 1919 and 1946 (and without taking into account the 1975 extension of the vote to 18 year olds), the size of the Italian electorate went from little more than 2 per cent of its inhabitants to about 60 per cent. Second, with the changeover from monarchy to republic, even the supreme position in the state became an elective one and therefore, in the technical sense of the word, representative. A nominated senate was replaced by a second chamber elected by universal suffrage. With the institution of regions with legislative power, an attempt was made to redistribute power from the centre to the periphery although it is too early to judge whether this has been successful. Finally, the recognition granted to all citizens of 'the right to associate freely in political parties and to compete democratically to determine national policy' (Article 49) was meant to legitimate organizations which facilitate the formation of a collective will through the aggregation of homogeneous interests in a society characterized by plurality of groups and strong social tensions.

The consolidation of representative democracy has not precluded the return of direct democracy, albeit in secondary forms. It could even be said that the ideal of direct democracy has never completely died out and has survived in radical political groups which have always tended to consider representative democracy not as an inevitable adaptation of the principle of popular sovereignty to the requirements of large states, but as a shameful and mistaken deviation from the original idea of government by the people, for the people and through the people. As is well known, Marx believed that several intimations of direct democracy were brought together in the brief experience of political government which was found in the Paris Commune between March and April of 1871. The theme was strongly taken up again by Lenin in *State and Revolution* (1917), an essay which was meant to have guided the mind and behaviour of the constructors of the new state which was rising from the ashes of Tsarist autocracy. Direct democracy is often contrasted, as the real form of socialist democracy, with representative democracy which is condemned as truncated and deceitful and, moreover, the only form of democracy possible in a class state such as the bourgeois state. By direct democracy is meant all those forms of participation in power which do not constitute any kind of representation (neither the representation of general and political interests nor the representation of particular and organic interests): that is, (a) government by the people through delegates with specified and revocable mandates; (b) government by an assembly (namely, government not only without irrevocable or mandated representatives, but also without delegates); (c) referendum.

The first of these is found in the present Soviet Constitution, whose Article 142 says that 'every deputy is accountable to the electorate for his own work and for the work of the Soviet of workers' deputies, and may be recalled at any moment by a majority decision of the electorate.' In most constitutions of popular democracies, the second form usually belongs to an emerging phase of collective movements, the so-called 'birth phase' which precedes institutionalization; recent examples are the stud-

· ent movement and the local council committees in large cities. The third form was inserted into some post-war constitutions like the Italian (Article 75). Of these three forms of direct democracy the second and third cannot hope to substitute and, indeed, they never have substituted the various forms of representative democracy practicable in a democratic state; just as the various forms of representative democracy have never pretended to substitute and, in fact, never have substituted authoritarian forms of exercising power as, for example, modes of bureaucratic organization in those states which are called democratic. Therefore on their own they cannot constitute a true and proper alternative to the representative state: the second because it is only applicable in small communities and the third because it is applicable only in exceptional circumstances of limited relevance. As for the first, with the formation of large party organizations which sometimes impose very strict voting discipline on the representatives elected on their policies, the difference between a representative with a mandate and one without becomes more and more blurred. The deputy elected through a party organization receives a mandate not from the electorate but from the party which punishes the deputy by revoking that mandate when he or she ignores discipline, which becomes a functional replacement for the electorate's imperative mandate.

POLITICAL DEMOCRACY AND SOCIAL DEMOCRACY

The enlargement of democracy in contemporary society occurs not only through the integration of representative and direct democracy but also (and above all) through the extension of democracy beyond politics to other spheres (democratization being understood as the institution and exercise of procedures which allow the participation of those affected in the deliberations of a collective body). If one democratic trend is to be seen nowadays it is not, as is often mistakenly maintained, the substitution of direct democracy for representative democracy (which is, in any case, impossible in large organizations), but the transfer of democracy from the political sphere (where the individual is regarded as a citizen) to the social sphere (where the individual is regarded as many-faceted); for example, as father and son; as spouse; as entrepreneur and worker; as teacher and student and student's parent; as officer and soldier; as administrator and client; as producer and consumer; as manager of public utilities, and so on. In other words, in the extension of the form of ascending power (which up until now was confined to the larger political associations) to the arena of civil society in its various manifestations from the school to the work-place. Consequently, current forms of democratic development cannot be interpreted as the affirmation of a new type of democracy. Rather, they should be understood as the occupation of new spaces, which up to now have been dominated by bureaucratic and hierarchical organizations, by some of the traditional forms of democracy.

Once the right to political participation has been achieved, a citizen of the most advanced democracies takes account of the fact that the political sphere has now been included in a much larger sphere, that of society as a whole; political decisions are conditioned, even determined, by what happens in the social sphere. This is why the democratization of political affairs, which occurs with the institution of parliament, goes hand-in-hand with the democratization of society. Consequently, it is perfectly possible to have a democratic state in a society where most institutions, from the family to school, and from the firm to public services, are not governed democratically. At this point the question arises that characterizes, better than any other, the actual state of development in countries which have the most politically advanced democracy: 'Is the survival of a democratic state possible in an undemocratic society?' This can also be formulated as follows: 'A political democracy was and still is necessary so that people are not governed despotically. But is it enough?' In recent times, when one wanted to give proof of the development of democracy in a given country, what mattered was the extent of political rights, from restricted to universal suffrage; but no further development is possible once suffrage has been extended almost everywhere to women, and in some countries the age limit has been reduced to 18 years. Today, if you want an indication of the development of democracy in a country, you must consider not just the number of people with the right to vote, but also the number of different places besides the traditional area of politics in which the right to vote is exercised. In other words, to pass a judgement today on the development of democracy in a given country the question must be asked, not 'Who votes?' but 'On what issues can one vote?'

FORMAL DEMOCRACY AND SUBSTANTIVE DEMOCRACY

The discussion about the meaning of democracy will not be complete unless it takes account of the fact that there is another meaning to the word. Until now democracy has been considered as a complex of institutions characterized by the type of answer given to two questions: 'Who governs?' and 'How is government exercised?' However, there is another meaning of the word 'democracy' in modern political language: a regime characterized by certain ends and values towards whose realization a certain political group aims and works. Behind these ends and values, which are used to distinguish a democratic from an undemocratic regime not just formally but substantially, lies the principle of equality. This is understood not as the legal equality introduced into liberal constitutions when they were not even formally democratic but as social and, at least in part, economic equality. Thus there is a distinction between formal democracy, dealing with the form of government, and substantive democracy which deals with the content of this form. These two meanings are found perfectly fused in the Rousseauistic theory of democracy, since the egalitarian ideal which inspires it is realized in the formation of the general will, and in view of this both meanings are historically legitimate. This historical legitimacy, however, does not license the belief that they refer to the same thing in spite of the identical terminology. It is even true historically that formal democracy fails to maintain the main promises of the substantive democratic programme and, similarly, substantive democracy operates through the undemocratic exercise of power. The sterility of the debate about to what degree regimes, which abide either by the principle of government by the people or government for the people, are democratic is proof of the lack of a common referential element. Every regime is democratic according to the meaning of democracy presumed by its defendants, and undemocratic in the sense upheld by its detractors. The only point on which both sides agree is that the perfect democracy should be both substantively and formally democratic. But this type of regime up to now has never existed.

ANCIENT DICTATORSHIP

As democracy came to be considered the best (or least bad) form of government – the form best suited to the most socially, economically and politically developed societies – the evaluative use of the theory of governmental forms simplified the traditional typology and became polarized, as already said, around the dichotomy of democracy/autocracy. In common use, however, the usual term for the second part of the dichotomy is not 'autocracy' but 'dictatorship'. Today the use of the term 'dictatorship' is so widespread for governments which are not democracies and which have arisen by suppressing preceding democracies that the technically more correct term 'autocracy' has been relegated to manuals of public law. The present great dichotomy is not an opposition of democracy and autocracy but of democracy and dictatorship, even if the second term is used in a historically incorrect manner. The use of the term 'dictatorship' to refer to all non-democratic regimes became widespread after the First World War, both in the heated debate on the form of government established by the Bolsheviks and in the descriptions of fascist regimes, beginning with the Italian, which were employed by their opponents. This opposition of dictatorship to democracy within a system of discourse where democracy came to have a eulogistic meaning ended up by imputing to 'dictatorship' a negative meaning which was contrary to its historical usage and which really belonged in classical philosophy to other terms such as 'tyranny' and 'despotism' and, more recently, 'autocracy'. Even in 1936, Elie Halévy could define his own times as 'the age of tyranny', but today this expression is no longer used to define the 20 years between the two world wars: the regimes that Halévy called 'tyrannies' have passed into history as 'dictatorships'.

'Dictatorship' is a term which, like 'tyranny', 'despotism' and 'autocracy', derives from classical antiquity. However, it differs from them in having had originally and for centuries a positive connotation. 'Dictator' was the name of the office of an extraordinary Roman magistrate, which was instituted in about 500 BC and lasted until the end of the third century AD. He was nominated by one of the consuls under exceptional circumstances such as the conduct of a war (*dictator rei publicae gerundae causa*) or the suppression of a revolt (*dictator seditionis sedandae causa*) and because of the exceptional situation he was given extraordinary powers. These consisted above all in the decreasing distinction between the *imperium domi*, which was the sovereign command exercised within the city walls and consequently subject to such constitutional limits as *provacatio ad populum*, and the *imperium militiae*, which was the military power exercised outside the walls and as such was not subject to constitutional limits. The excessive power of the dictator was counterbalanced by its temporary nature: the dictator was nominated only for the duration of the extraordinary task entrusted to him, for a maximum period of six months, and never beyond the tenure of office of the consul who appointed him. The dictator, therefore, was an extraordinary magistrate but a legitimate one because his existence was foreseen by the constitution and his power justified by the state of necessity (the state of necessity is a normative fact according to lawyers; that is, a fact suitable for suspending an existing legal state and putting into action a new legal situation). In short, the characteristics of the Roman dictatorship were: (a) a legitimating state of necessity; (b) full powers of command; (c) one person alone invested with this command; (d) short duration of the office. In so far as it was a monocratic magistrature with extraordinary but limited and temporary powers, dictatorship is always distinct from tyranny and despotism with which, in current usage, it is often confused. The tyrant is a monocrat who exercises absolute power, but is neither legitimate nor necessarily temporary. The despot is a monocrat who exercises absolute power and is legitimate but not temporary (it may even be a long-term regime as demonstrated by the classic example of oriental despotism). What is common to these three forms is that they are filled by monocrats with absolute power; tyranny and dictatorship differ because, whilst the latter is legitimate, the former is not; despotism and dictatorship differ because, although they are both legitimate, the legitimacy of the first has a historico-geographical foundation while the second is legitimated by a state of necessity. Dictatorship differs from both tyranny and despotism by being temporary.

It was precisely this temporary character which earned dictatorship its favourable judgement from the great political writers. In a chapter of the *Discourses*, significantly entitled 'Dictatorial authority aided not damaged the Roman republic', Machiavelli refutes those who had maintained that dictatorship caused 'Rome's period of tyranny' (1513–19) because tyranny (the reference is to Caesar) was not brought about by dictatorship but by the prolongation of the dictatorship beyond the established limits. And he sees acutely that the positive aspect of dictatorship lay in its temporary and specific nature:

The Dictator was made to be temporary and not permanent and only in order to remedy the reason for his creation; and his authority included the power to decide for himself remedies to that pressing danger, to act without consultation and to punish without appeal; but he could not do anything that would diminish the state or that would reduce the authority of the Senate or the People, to unmake the old orders of the city and make new ones.

In the *Social Contract*, after observing that the law could not possibly foresee all possible cases and that exceptional cases would occur in which it would be momentarily expedient to suspend their effect, Rousseau states that, 'In these rare and obvious cases public security is provided for by a particular act entrusting the office to him who is most worthy' (1762). This delegation can occur in two ways: either by increasing the authority of the legitimate government, in which case the authority of the laws is not changed, only the form of their administration; or, when the danger is such that the system of laws might constitute a barrier to resolute action, by nominating a supreme chief (the dictator) who 'silences all laws and momentarily suspends sovereign authority' (Rousseau 1762). For Rousseau, too, dictatorship is healthy only if it is strictly limited in time: 'In whatever manner this important trust is conferred, its duration should be fixed at a very short period which in no circumstances should be prolonged . . . because once the urgent need has passed dictatorship becomes tyrannical or useless' (1762).

MODERN DICTATORSHIP

It is clear from the history of this office and from classic interpretations that the dictator exercises extraordinary powers but only in the area of the executive function and not the legislative one. Machiavelli and Rousseau equally emphasized this limitation, the former writing, as we have seen, that the dictator was not able to do anything that might 'diminish the state', the other that 'the suspension of legislative activity' (which was due to the dictator) 'in no way abolished it', because 'the magistrate who silences it cannot make it speak' (Rousseau 1762). Only in modern times, the age of the great revolutions, has the concept of dictatorship been extended to the establishing power of the new order: that is, to revolutionary power which, to follow Machiavelli, unravels the old order with the aim of establishing a new one. In his noted work on dictatorship (1921), Carl Schmitt distinguishes between classic dictatorship which he calls, quoting from Bodin, 'commissary' (in the sense that the dictator executes his extraordinary task within the limits of the commission received), and the dictatorship of modern or revolutionary times, which he calls 'sovereign' and which 'sees in all existing order a state of affairs to be entirely removed through its own action' and therefore 'does not usurp an existing constitution but rather aims at a state of affairs in which it is possible to impose an authentic constitution'.

Revolutionary dictatorship also springs from a state of necessity and temporarily exercises exceptional powers (at least in the initial intention), and for this reason it is given the name of dictatorship, but the task attributed to it and which it takes on itself is much vaster. It is no longer a question of remedying a partial crisis of the state, such as an external war or a revolt, but of resolving a total crisis, a crisis that throws into doubt the very existence of a given regime, such as a civil war (that is, a war that can signal the end of the old order and the birth of a new one). The dictator has been invested with his power by the constitution and has, therefore, a constituted power, whereas the sovereign dictator invests himself with power or receives a merely symbolic popular investiture, and assumes a constituting power. The French National Convention, which decided on 10 October 1793 to suspend the Constitution of the same year (never to be restored), and which established a provisional revolutionary government until the arrival of peace is an exemplary case of the second type of dictatorship. Compared to classical dictatorship, the Jacobin dictator is no longer a monocratic magistrate – even if the personality of Robespierre is conspicuous – but is the dictatorship of a revolutionary group: the Committee of Public Health.

The dissociation of the concept of dictatorship from the concept of monocratic power must be emphasized because it marks the passage from the classic use of the term, which after the revolution even applied to Napoleon's regime which was interpreted as a military dictatorship, to the modern use popularized through the writings of Marx and Engels. Used in expressions such as the 'dictatorship of the bourgeoisie' and the 'dictatorship of the proletariat', the term referred not to a person, or even a group of people, but to an entire class. Even if its original meaning was much tampered with it could be gainfully replaced by the term 'domination' as used in the typically Marxist and Engelian expression 'class domination'. Moreover, what distinguishes the character of the modern dictatorship from its classical form is the extension of power which is no longer limited to the executive function but is extended to the legislative and even constitutive functions, even if the specific case of the French Revolutionary Government tended to present itself as not abolishing but as suspending exceptionally and provisionally the constitution and, therefore, as a dictatorship in the classical sense of the word. In reality, the difference beteween revolutionary (similarly counterrevolutionary) and commissary dictatorship reveals itself not in the declarations of the principles, who never fail to solemnly announce their temporariness, but in the facts: that is, the effects produced on the preceding order.

REVOLUTIONARY DICTATORSHIP

Another step forward in the history of the fate of the concept of dictatorship is that made by the unfortunate standard-bearers of an egalitarian revolution (which, in fact, never took place): Babeuf, Buonarroti and comrades, the protagonists of the Conspiracy of Equals (9–10 September 1795). In the thinking of these men, especially of Buonarroti who, having survived the condemnation of his comrades, in the last years of his long life became the historian and theorist of the conspiracy in his book *Conspiration pour l'égalité dite de Babeuf* (1828), the idea is clearly stated that the revolution must be achieved by a handful of motivated men. There must follow after the explosion of the revolution a transitory state marked by the exercise of exceptional powers concentrated in the hands of a few (a genuine precedent for Marx's and Lenin's state of transition) and that, finally, the new society of equals should only be installed after the revolutionary dictatorship has succeeded in eliminating not only the oppressors of the people but also those 'considered incapable of regenerating themselves', as well as every vestige of the past, using violence if necesssary. Buonarroti wrote that to overcome the difficulties present after the revolution, the strength of all would be necesssary but that this strength would be nothing 'if not directed by a strong, consistent, enlightened and immutable will' and that 'many reforms would be necessary before the general will could emanate and be recognised' (1828–9). One of the tasks attributed by Buonarroti to the revolutionary government of 'wise men' is the preparation of the new constitution which would complete the revolutionary phase, thus demonstrating beyond any shadow of doubt that the salient characteristic of the revolutionary dictatorship is the exercise of sovereign power *par excellence*: that is, constitutive power.

It must be emphasized that in this new context dictatorship, although having changed its descriptive meaning, has lost nothing of the positive value of the original. In contrast to the current use which compares dictatorship unfavourably with democracy, the first use of 'dictatorship' to denote revolutionary dictatorship as well as military dictatorship shares the favour enjoyed by the Roman magistracy, summoned in exceptional situations to save the republic from war or rebellion, and the term was used again with a favourable connotation. It should also be remembered that in the seventeenth century the term 'despotism' was used for the first time with a positive sense in the distinction made by the physiocrat Le Mercier de la Rivière between arbitrary despotism, 'founded on the opinion which lends itself to all the disorders and all the excesses to which ignorance makes it susceptible', and legal despotism, 'established naturally and necessarily by law', and was therefore understood as the best form of government which – precisely because of the monocratic and absolute nature of its power – was capable of reading dispassionately and perfectly the great book of nature and of declaring and applying the laws that must regulate the social order. It was enough to use the term 'enlightened' to change the value of even such a 'despotism' which had been execrated for centuries. When Buonarroti called the will of the committee of bold men who must guide the revolution 'enlightened', and the components of the government in the state of transition 'wise', he invites us to line up the idea of revolutionary dictatorship with that of enlightened despotism. The idea of revolutionary dictatorship as a provisional and temporary government imposed by exceptional circumstances survived in the theory and practice of Blanqui rather than Marx. Marx's political theory speaks of dictatorship of the proletariat in the sense of domination by a class not of a committee, and even less of a party; he does not, therefore, use the sense that the term had substantially preserved in the passage from classical dictatorship to modern dictatorship. The only remarks made by Marx on the state of transition deal with the experience of the Paris Commune between March and May 1871, and argue that the government of the Commune represented a more advanced form of democracy than the representative democracy of the most advanced bourgeois states. Nothwithstanding this Engels, in his preface to Marx's writings on the civil war in France, saw in the Paris Commune the first great and terrible trial of the dictatorship of the proletariat.

But this makes even more evident the fact that class domination (dictatorship in the non-technical sense) is one thing and the form of government in which this domination expresses itself is another (and the case of the Commune was not, at least in Marx's interpretation, a dictatorship in the technical sense).

In the Marxian expression 'dictatorship of the proletariat' the term 'dictatorship' has no particular evaluative significance: since all states are dictatorships, in the sense of domination by a class, the term refers substantially to a state of affairs and has an essentially descriptive significance. The shift from dictatorship with a positive value, referring to a magistracy or a revolutionary government, to the negative value which is prevalent today, occurred because the term no longer indicates generically the dominion of a class but a form of government: that is, a mode of exercising power. The term now extends to all undemocratic ways of wielding power and it loses all its specific connotations in this enlargement, above all the state of necessity and of temporariness which was used to justify the many positive evaluations of this institution (the Roman dictatorship) and of a form of government modelled on it (revolutionary dictatorship).

Bibliography

Almond, G.A. and Powell, G.B., 1966, *Comparative Politics. A Developmental Approach*, Little & Brown, Boston.

Althusius, J., 1603, *Politica methodice digesta exemplis sacris et profanis illustrata*, second edition, Herborn 1614; ed. cit. Harvard University Press, Cambridge (Mass.) 1932 (tr. *The Politics of Johannes Althusius*, Eyre and Spottiswode, London 1965).

Anonymous, 1765a, *Société (Morale)*, in *Encyclopédie, -ou Dictionnaire raisonné des sciences, des arts et des métiers, par une société de gens de lettres. Mis en ordre et publié par M. Diderot . . . , et quant à la Partie Mathématique, par M. d'Alembert . . .* , Briasson, David, Le Breton, Durand, Paris 1751–65, vol. XV, pp. 252–8 (*anthology*).

——1765b, *Société civile*, ibid., p. 259.

Böckenförde, E.W. (ed.), 1976, *Staat und Gesellschaft*, Wissenschaftliche Buchgesellschaft, Darmstadt.

Bodin, J., 1576, *Les Six livres de la République*, Du Puys, Paris (tr. *The Six Books of a Commonweale*, Arno, New York 1979).

Bucharin, N.I. and Preobraženskij, E.A., 1919, *Azbuka Kommunizma*, Moscow (tr. *The ABC of Communism*, Socialist Labour Press, Glasgow 1921).

Buonarroti, F., 1828, *Conspiration pour l'égalité dite de Babeuf*, Librairie romantique, Brussels.

——(1828–9) (Sui caratteri del governo rivoluzionario), manuscript fragment published in A. Galante Garrone, *Filippo Buonarroti e i rivoluzionari dell'Ottocento (1828–1837)*, Einaudi, Turin 1951.

Burke, E., 1790, *Reflections on the Revolution in France*, Dodsley, London.

Croce, B., 1925, *Politica in nuce*, in *Elementi di politica*, Laterza, Bari; also in *Etica e politica*, Laterza, Bari 1954, pp. 217–54.

Dahl, R.A., 1963, *Modern Political Analysis*, Prentice-Hall, Englewood Cliffs (NJ).

Elia, L., 1970, *Governo (forme di)*, in *Enciclopedia del diritto*, vol. XIX, Giuffrè, Milan, pp. 63–75.

Evans-Pritchard, E.E. and Fortes, M. (ed.), 1940, *African Political Systems*, Oxford University Press, London.

Farneti, P., 1973, Introduzione a P. Farneti (ed.), *Il sistema politico italiano*, Il Mulino, Bologna, pp. 7–60.

Filmer, R., 1680, *Patriarcha. Or the Natural Power of Kings*, Chiswell, London.

Gramsci, A., (1930–2a), *Passato e presente. I cattolici e lo Stato*, in *Quaderni del carcere*, Einaudi, Turin 1975, pp. 662–3 (tr. *Selections from the Prison Notebooks of Antonio Gramsci*, Lawrence and Wishart, London 1971).

——(1930–2b), *Armi e religione*, ibid., pp. 762–3.

——(1932), *Appunti e nôte sparse per un gruppo di saggi sulla storia degli intellettuali, ibid.*, pp. 1511–51.

Grotius, U., 1625, *De iure Belli ac Pacis libri tres*, Buon, Paris.

Gurvitch, G., 1944, *La déclaration des droits sociaux*, Editions de la Maison française, New York; ed. cit. Vrin, Paris 1946.

Habermas, J., 1964, *Offentlichkeit*, in *Fischer-Lexikon*, II. *Staat und Politik*, Fischer Bücherei, Frankfurt am Main-Hamburg 1957; also in *Kultur und Kritik*, Suhrkamp, Frankfurt am Main, pp. 61–9 (tr. 'The Public Sphere: An Encyclopaedia Article', *New German Critique*, 1974, no. 3).

Haller, K.L. von, 1816, *Restauration der Staats-Wissenschaft, oder Theorie des natürlichgesellingen Zustands der Chimäre des Künstlich-bürgerlichen entgegengesetzi*, vol. I, Steiner, Winterthur.

Hamilton, A., Jay, J. and Madison J., (1787–8), *The Federalist*, MacLean, New York 1788.

Hegel, G.W.F., (1799–1802), *Kritik der Verfasssung Deutschlands*, Fischer, Kassel 1893.

——(1808–12), *Philosophische Propädeutik*, Duncker und Humblot, Berlin 1840 (tr. *The Philosophical Propaedeutic*, Basil Blackwell, Oxford 1986).

——1821, *Grundlinien der Philosophie des Rechts*, Nicolai, Berlin (tr. *The Philosophy of Right*, Oxford University Press, London 1942).

——(1830–1), *Vorlesungen über die Philosophie der Geschichte*, Frommann, Stuttgart 1934 (tr. *Lectures on the Philosophy of*

History, New York 1956).

Hobbes, Thomas, 1642, *Elementorum Philosophiae, Sectio Tertia. De Cive*, Elzevier, Amsterdam 1647.

——1651, *Leviathan, or the Matter, Form, and Power of a Common-wealth, Ecclesiasticall and Civill*, Crooke, London.

Jellinek, G., 1911, *Allgemeine Staatslehre*, Häring, Berlin.

Kant, I., 1796, *Zum ewigen Frieden. Ein philosophischer Entwurf*, Nicolovius, Königsberg (tr. *Perpetual Peace*, in *Kant's Political Writings*, Cambridge University Press, Cambridge 1977).

——1797, *Die Metaphysik der Sitten*, I. *Metaphysische Anfangsgründe der Rechtslehre*, Nicolovius, Königsberg (tr. *Metaphysics of Morals. Part 1. The Metaphysical Elements of Justice*, Bobbs-Merrill, New York 1965).

Kelsen, H., 1922, *Der soziologische und der juristische Staatsbegriff. Kritische Untersuchung des Verhältnissses von Staat und Recht*, Mohr, Tübingen.

——1945, *General Theory of Law and State*, Harvard University Press, Cambridge (Mass.).

——1960, *Reine Rechtslebre*, Deuticke, Vienna 1960 (tr. *The Pure Theory of Law*, University of California Press, Berkeley 1967).

Lasswell, H.D. and Kaplan, A., 1952, *Power and Society. A Framework for Political Inquiry*, Routledge and Kegan Paul, London 1952.

Lenin, V.I., (1917), *Gosudarstvo i revoljucija*, Žizn' i Znanie, Petrograd 1918 (tr. *The State and Revolution*, Allen and Unwin, London 1919).

Locke, J., 1690, *Two Treatises of Government*, Churchill, London.

——1694, *An Essay on Human Understanding*, Ballet, London.

Luhmann, N., 1972, *Rechtssoziologie*, Rowohlt, Hamburg (tr. *A Sociological Theory of Law*, Routledge and Kegan Paul, London 1985).

Luther, M., 1523, *Von welltlicher uberkeytt, wie weytt man yhr gehorsam schuldig sey*, Schyrlentz, Wittenberg.

Machiavelli, N., (1513), *Il Principe*, Blado, Roma-Giunta, Firenze 1532; ed. cit. Einaudi, Turin 1977 (tr. *The Prince*, Penguin, Harmondsworth 1975).

——(1513–19), *Discorsi sopra la prima decca di Tito Livio*, Blado, Rome-Giunta, Florence 1531; ed. cit. Feltrinelli, Milan 1977 (tr. *The Discourses*, Penguin, Harmondsworth 1970).

Marx, K., (1843), *Zur Judenfrage*, in 'Deutsch-Französische Jahrbücher', n. 1 (1844) (tr. *On the Jewish Question*, in *Early*

Writings, L. Colletti (ed.), London 1975).

——1859, *Zur-Kritik der politischen Ökonomie,* Duncker, Berlin (tr. *A Critique of Political Economy,* in *Marx and Engels: Selected Works,* Moscow 1935).

——and Engels, F., 1845, *Die heilige Familie, oder Kritik der kritischen Kritik. Gegen Bruno Bauer und Consorten,* Rütten, Frankfurt am Main (tr. *The Holy Family,* Moscow 1956).

Montesquieu, C.-L. de Secondat de, 1734, *Considérations sur les causes de la grandeur des Romains et de leur décadence,* Desbordes, Amsterdam.

——1748, *De l'Esprit des loix. . .,* Barrillot et fils, Geneva (*tr. Spirit of the Laws,* University of California Press, Berkeley 1978).

More, T., 1516, *De optimo reipublicae statu deque nova insula Utopia,* Martens, Louvain (tr. *Utopia,* Dent, London 1974).

Mortati, C., 1969, *Istituzioni di diritto pubblico,* Cedam, Padua 1969.

Mosca, G., 1896, *Elementi di scienza politica,* Bocca, Rome; ed. cit. Laterza, Bari 1923 (tr. *The Ruling Class,* McGraw-Hill, New York 1939).

——1933, *Storia delle dottrine politiche,* Laterza, Bari 1937.

Nozick, R., 1974, *Anarchy, State and Utopia,* Basic Books, New York.

Paine, Thomas, 1776, *Common Sense, Addressed to the Inhabitants of America,* Phoenix, Baltimore.

Pašukanis, E.B., 1924, *Obŝĉaja teorija prava i marksizm,* Izdatel'stvo Kommunistiĉeskoi Akademii, Moscow 1927.

Pufendorf, S., 1672, *De iure naturae et gentium,* Haberegger, London.

Radbruch, G., 1932, *Rechtsphilosophie,* Quelle und Meyer, Leipzig.

Rawls, J., 1971, *A Theory of Justice,* The Belknap Press of Harvard University Press, Cambridge (Mass.).

Rosmini-Serbati, A., 1841–3, *Filosofia del diritto,* 2 vols., Boniardini-pogliani, Milan; ed. cit. Cedam, Padua 1967–9.

Rousseau, J.-J., 1762, *Du contrat social,* Rey, Amsterdam (tr. *The Social Contract,* Dent, London 1973).

Russell, B., 1938, *Power. A New Social Analysis,* Allen and Unwin, London.

Schmitt, C., 1921, *Die Diktatur,* Duncker und Humblot, Berlin-Leipzig.

——1928, *Verfassungslehre*, Duncker und Humblot, Munich-Leipzig.

Spinoza, B., 1670, *Tractatus theologico-politicus*, Künraht, Hamburg (tr. *A Theological–Political Treatise*, Dover, New York 1951).

Tocqueville, A. de, 1835–40, *De la démocratie en Amérique*, Gosselin, Paris (tr. *Democracy in America*, New American Library, New York 1956).

——1848, *Avertissement de la douzième édition* in *De la démocratie en Amérique*, Pagnerre, Paris 1848.

Treitschke, H. von, (1894–6), *Politik. Vorlesungen gehalten an der Universität zu Berlin*, Hirzel, Leipzig 1897–8 (tr. *Politics*, Constable and Co., London 1916).

Vico, G., 1720, *De universi iuris uno principio et uno fine*, in *Il diritto universale*, Laterza, Bari 1936.

——1744, *La Scienza nuova giusta l'edizione del 1744*, Laterza, Bari 1967 (tr. *The New Science*, Cornell University Press, Ithaca NY 1948).

Weber, M., (1908–20), *Wirtschaft und Gesellschaft. Grundriss der verstehenden Soziologie*, Mohr, Tübingen 1922 (tr. *Economy and Society: An Outline of Interpretative Sociology*, University of California Press, Berkeley 1978).

Index

Index by Ann Hall